CONCISE GUIDES

ALEXANDER THE GREAT – ONE MAN. ONE EMPIRE, ONE LEGACY

Empires Created, Cultures Transformed, Legends Created. The Story of One of the Greatest Military Commanders in History.

James Burrows

© **Copyright 2025 - All rights reserved.**

The content contained within this book may not be reproduced, duplicated or transmitted without direct written permission from the author or the publisher.

Under no circumstances will any blame or legal responsibility be held against the publisher, or author, for any damages, reparation, or monetary loss due to the information contained within this book, either directly or indirectly.

Legal Notice:

This book is copyright protected. It is only for personal use. You cannot amend, distribute, sell, use, quote or paraphrase any part, or the content within this book, without the consent of the author or publisher.

Disclaimer Notice:

Please note the information contained within this document is for educational and entertainment purposes only. All effort has been executed to present accurate, up to date, reliable, complete information. No warranties of any kind are declared or implied. Readers acknowledge that the author is not engaged in the rendering of legal, financial, medical or professional advice. The content within this book has been derived from various sources. Please consult a licensed professional before attempting any techniques outlined in this book.

By reading this document, the reader agrees that under no circumstances is the author responsible for any losses, direct or indirect, that are incurred as a result of the use of the information contained within this document, including, but not limited to, errors, omissions, or inaccuracies.

Other Books by James Burrows

What You Need To Know:

World War I for Teens
World War I for Kids
World War II for Teens
World War II for Kids
World War II for Teens – 21 Special Operations
World War II for Teens – The Secret War
World War II for Teens – The Holocaust
World War II – The Pacific War
The Vietnam War for Teens

The Ultimate Guide:

Egyptian Mythology for Kids
Greek Mythology for Kids
Norse Mythology for Kids

Concise Guides:

A History of Israel and Palestine
Alexander the Great - One Man. One Empire. One Legacy.

Other Books:

The Art of War – Sun Tzu
Meditations – Marcus Aurelius

CONTENTS

PROLOGUE

TIMELINE OF KEY EVENTS

Part I: Origins of a Conqueror

Chapter 1: The World Before Alexander

Chapter 2: Childhood and Education

Chapter 3: Prince to King

Part II: Conquest of an Empire

Chapter 4: The Persian Campaign Begins

Chapter 5: Defeating Darius III

Chapter 6: Into Egypt

Part III: At the Edge of the World

Chapter 7: Across Central Asia

Chapter 8: The Indian Campaign

Part IV: The Final Chapter

Chapter 9: Return Through Hardship

Chapter 10: Death in Babylon

Part V: The World After Alexander

Chapter 11: The Wars of the Successors

Chapter 12: The Hellenistic Age

Part VI: Legacy and Legend

Chapter 13: Military Genius

Chapter 14: Myth and Memory

Chapter 15: Final Reflections

EPILOGUE: A DREAM THAT OUTLIVED ITS DREAMER

APPENDIX

- Glossary of People, Places and Terms
- Quotes Attributed to Alexander
- Cities Founded and Named After Alexander

ABOUT THE AUTHOR

PROLOGUE – THE KING AT BABYLON

The desert sun hung low over the Euphrates as Alexander rode into Babylon. He was thirty-one years old, and the world, as much of it as had ever been known to the Greeks, lay behind him, subdued. Dust clung to the polished bronze of his armor. Around him stretched an army weathered by war and time: Macedonians who had marched with him for a decade, Persians newly adopted into the ranks, and men from every nation and tongue he had conquered along the way. Trumpets sounded. Crowds lined the streets. Priests emerged from the temples with garlands and incense. In this ancient city of kings, a greater king had returned.

Bust of Alexander the Great in the collections of the Istanbul Archaeological Museums

Babylon, the ancient jewel of Mesopotamia, was his now. Once the seat of mighty Nebuchadnezzar, and before that Hammurabi, it had welcomed conquerors before. But none like this. Alexander of Macedon entered the city not just as a general or monarch, but as a living myth, a man whose footsteps had traced the edge of the known world, whose ambition outpaced the reach of his own empire, and whose very name had become a word of awe.

It was spring in 324 BC. The campaigns were over, for now. His last battle had been fought months earlier on the banks of the Hydaspes, far to the east in the rich plains of the Punjab. The vast armies of Persia had long since been broken. Darius III was dead, and the once-proud Achaemenid Empire lay in ruins. Egypt hailed him as pharaoh. The Greeks, once his skeptical peers, now spoke of him in reverent tones. And still, Alexander was not finished.

In Babylon, plans were already forming. He would launch a fleet to Arabia, then to Carthage. Perhaps even to Rome. He would govern from the center of the world, a city of gardens and ziggurats, of gods and merchants, of soldiers and scribes. Babylon would be the capital of a new, united world, Greek and Persian, East and West, held together not by tyranny but by vision.

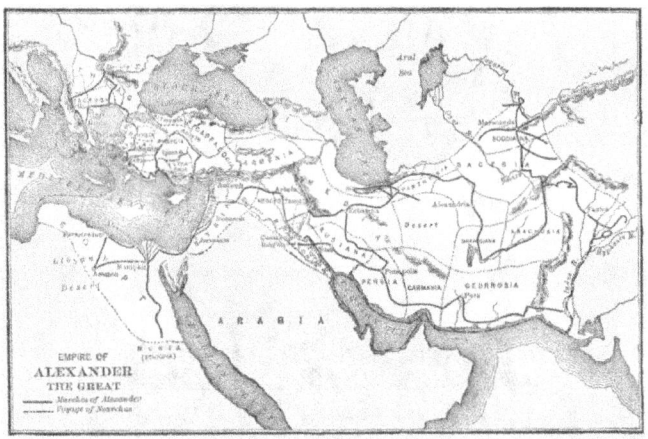

Alexander the Great's Empire, from Greece to the Indian Subcontinent

But beneath the triumph and the gold, there was unease. The empire was vast, but its unity was fragile. The veterans were weary. The generals whispered. The eastern peoples remained unsure whether this Macedonian king was their liberator or a new Darius in foreign clothes. And Alexander himself, for all his glory, carried the weight of ghosts.

He had seen friends die. He had buried men he loved. He had been wounded more than once, and in the deserts of Gedrosia, he had lost nearly half his army to thirst and heat. In his eyes was the glint not just of destiny, but of something darker, a man chasing something he could never quite reach, driven by gods, omens, and the endless roar of his own name.

He had built the largest empire the world had yet known. But now, back in Babylon, Alexander faced a challenge no sword could conquer.

What now?

The Distance Traveled

Ten years earlier, he had been just a boy of twenty, newly crowned king of Macedon after the assassination of his father, Philip II. He had inherited a formidable military and a bold political vision, but he had also inherited a fragile kingdom, rebellious Greek city-states, and the lingering menace of Persia looming across the Aegean.

To most observers, Alexander seemed too young, too brash, too inexperienced. Few believed he could hold Macedonia together, let alone lead it to glory. And yet, within two years, he had crossed the Hellespont into Asia Minor, stood victorious on the banks of the Granicus, and begun a campaign that would shake the very structure of the ancient world.

He defeated Darius III not once but three times, first at Issus, then at Gaugamela, and finally in the silent echo of the king's flight and murder. He burned Persepolis, humbled Babylon, and absorbed the wealth of Susa. He had reached Egypt and been proclaimed the son of Zeus-Ammon. He had stood before the Oracle at Siwa, seeking divine affirmation of his identity. He had walked the path of Achilles and tried to outshine even Heracles.

But it wasn't just the battles that defined him. Along the way, he had founded more than seventy cities, promoted intermarriage between Greeks and Persians, and elevated local elites in conquered regions. He dreamed not just of ruling the world, but of reshaping it, melding East and West into a new civilizational order.

This was no ordinary conqueror. This was a man trying to leave something eternal.

Ambition Beyond Conquest

In Babylon, as 324 BC unfolded, the vastness of Alexander's vision became more apparent, and more dangerous.

He had begun integrating Persian soldiers into his ranks, training them in Macedonian formations. He declared that all peoples in the empire, Greek, Persian, Egyptian, Indian, were equal under his rule. He demanded proskynesis, the Persian custom of bowing before the king, from his Greek companions, a step too far for many. Murmurs of discontent surfaced. Some questioned whether Alexander was still a Macedonian king or had become a Persian despot.

And yet, there was method to his boldness. Alexander believed in unity through inclusion, in an empire where culture was not suppressed but fused. At the mass weddings at Susa, he had arranged for thousands of his men to marry Persian women, symbolizing the blending of traditions. He himself had taken Roxana, a Sogdian princess, as his bride.

It was a grand experiment, perhaps the most audacious in history. But it came at a cost. His old comrades, men who had followed him from Pella and fought at his side across Asia, began to feel like strangers in their own army. Loyalty, once unquestioned, became complicated.

The empire was too vast, too young, too diverse. Holding it together required more than charisma, it required a new political order. Alexander was trying to build that order in Babylon.

But time was running short.

The Shadow of Mortality

Alexander had never feared death. He had charged into battle at the head of his cavalry, scaled walls, fought wounded, and dared the gods to strike him down. But now, in what would be the final year of his life, he began to sense the weight of what he could not control.

He had lost Hephaestion, his closest companion in the previous year. The grief had nearly broken him. He had mourned like Achilles weeping for Patroclus. He built temples in Hephaestion's honor, demanded hero-worship, and vowed to spread his name across the empire. But grief left a scar.

Alexander had always believed himself chosen, perhaps even divine. But now he began to ask: what if divinity wasn't enough? What if death came, not as a glorious moment in battle, but slowly, from within?

The days in Babylon were filled with planning. Maps were unrolled, ships outfitted, envoys dispatched. A new campaign, into Arabia, perhaps to Carthage, or even farther west, was being organized. But even amid the fever of ambition, there were signs. The rituals became more frequent. The consultations with soothsayers more intense. He had conquered the world, but the uncertainty of legacy haunted him.

Who would succeed him? His wife, Roxana, was pregnant, but the child, Alexander IV, had yet to be born. His half-brother, Philip Arrhidaeus, was mentally unfit to rule. His generals were loyal but ambitious, bound together only by Alexander's presence. And that presence, for all its fire, was mortal.

In June of 323 BC, Alexander fell ill.

A Life Beyond Life

The mystery of his death would fuel debate for centuries, fever, poison, disease, divine judgment. But one thing is certain: his death was not the end.

In many ways, it was only the beginning.

Alexander left no heir, no constitution, no clear succession plan. His empire fractured almost instantly. His generals turned on one another. His wife and son were murdered. His body was hijacked and buried in Alexandria, the Egyptian city he had founded but never ruled. His tomb became a place of pilgrimage, and eventually, disappeared.

And yet his influence only grew. The Hellenistic Age that followed saw Greek language, art, science, and philosophy spread from Egypt to India. The kingdoms carved from his empire, Ptolemaic Egypt, Seleucid Asia, Antigonid Macedon, blended Greek and local traditions into something entirely new.

He became a model for emperors: Julius Caesar wept at his statue. Napoleon carried his histories into battle. He appears in the Qur'an as Dhul-Qarnayn, in Persian legend as Iskander, in medieval romances as a knight-errant. He was no longer just a man. He was an idea, of greatness, ambition, and the price of immortality.

Themes of a Life

This book, Alexander the Great: Empire, Ambition, and Immortality, is not simply a retelling of campaigns and conquests. It is a story about vision, about how far one person can go, how much one mind can imagine, and what is gained or lost in the process.

At its heart lie several core themes:

- Ambition: Alexander's life was a constant push beyond limits, geographical, cultural, political, even divine. His ambition drove him from Macedon to the edges of India. But was it genius, or hubris?

- Conquest and Empire: Alexander was a destroyer and a builder. He razed cities and founded new ones. He overthrew dynasties and elevated local rulers. His empire was built in blood, but also in ideals. In his mind, he was not invading; he was transforming. But what did he truly seek to create?

- Cultural Fusion: Unlike many conquerors, Alexander tried to blend cultures, not erase them. His dream of unity between Greek and Persian, East and West, remains one of the most remarkable aspects of his legacy.

- Mortality and Legacy: For all his power, Alexander could not escape death. This is the paradox of his life: he achieved what no one else could yet left behind chaos. What does it mean to leave a mark on history?

A Man of His Time, and Ours

More than two millennia after his death, why does Alexander still matter?

Because he represents the eternal human struggle between greatness and destruction, between vision and vanity, between what we dream and what we can achieve. He was the ultimate explorer of the ancient world, not of oceans or stars, but of what a single life might accomplish.

He asked questions that still haunt us: Can we unite the world? Can one person change history? And at what cost?

In the chapters that follow, we will trace Alexander's journey from a teenage prince in Pella to a god-king in Babylon, from student to general, from man to myth. We will walk beside him through burning deserts and into royal courts, across battlefield dust and temple stone. We will see the glories, the betrayals, the wonders, and the end.

For Alexander's story is not just a story of conquest. It is a story about the limits of power, the shape of legacy, and the question that lies at the heart of every age:

What does it mean to be great?

TIMELINE OF KEY EVENTS

This timeline highlights the major milestones and key battles that shaped Alexander the Great's military campaigns and legacy.

356 BC: Birth of Alexander

- July 356 BC Alexander III is born in Pella, the capital of Macedonia, to King Philip II and Queen Olympias.

343 BC: Alexander's Education

- Aristotle, the philosopher, is appointed as Alexander's tutor. He provides Alexander with a broad education in philosophy, science, literature, and political theory.

340 BC: Alexander's First Military Experience

- At the age of 16, Alexander is left in charge of Macedon while his father goes on a military campaign. During this time, Alexander suppresses a rebellion by the Thracian tribe called the Maedi, and creates the city of Alexandropolis in the conquered territory.

338 BC: Battle of Chaeronea

- Alexander, at 18, fights in the Battle of Chaeronea alongside his father Philip II. The Macedonians defeat the Greek city-states of Athens and Thebes, solidifying Macedonian power in Greece.

336 BC: Assassination of Philip II

- King Philip II is assassinated. Alexander ascends to the throne of Macedon at the age of 20. He is quickly faced with revolts from Greek states, which he suppresses to secure his rule.

334 BC: Start of the Persian Campaign

- Alexander crosses the Hellespont (modern day Dardanelles in Turkey) into Asia Minor, marking the beginning of his campaign against the Persian Empire.

334 BC: Battle of the Granicus

- Alexander defeats a Persian army at the Battle of the Granicus River. This marks his first major victory over the Persians and secures western Anatolia.

333 BC: Battle of Issus

- Alexander defeats King Darius III of Persia at the Battle of Issus, despite being outnumbered. This victory secures Alexander's control over southern Asia Minor and puts him on a path toward Syria and Egypt.

332 BC: Siege of Tyre

- Alexander lays siege to the island city of Tyre. After a seven-month siege, he successfully captures the city, demonstrating his military ingenuity.

332 BC: Founding of Alexandria

- Alexander founds the city of Alexandria in Egypt, which becomes a major center of learning and culture in the ancient world.

331 BC: Battle of Gaugamela

- Alexander wins a decisive victory at the Battle of Gaugamela (also called the Battle of Arbela) against Darius III. This victory leads to the collapse of the Persian Empire and the conquest of Babylon, Susa, and Persepolis.

330 BC: Burning of Persepolis

- After the defeat of Darius III, Alexander marches into Persepolis, the Persian capital, and orders its destruction. The burning of Persepolis symbolizes the complete defeat of the Persian Empire and Alexander's triumph.

327 BC: Invasion of India

- Alexander crosses the Hindu Kush into India and begins his campaign in the Punjab region.

326 BC: Battle of the Hydaspes

- Alexander defeats King Porus of the Paurava kingdom at the Battle of the Hydaspes River. This battle is notable for its strategic complexity, the use of war elephants by the Indian army, and Alexander's ability to adapt to unfamiliar tactics.

325 BC: Mutiny at the Hyphasis River

- After the victory at Hydaspes, Alexander's army reaches the Hyphasis River (Beas River) in India. Exhausted by years of campaigning and unwilling to march further east, his troops mutiny and refuse to advance, forcing Alexander to turn back.

324 BC: Return to Babylon

- Alexander leads his army back toward Babylon. He faces harsh conditions in the Gedrosian Desert on the return journey, which takes a heavy toll on his men.

323 BC: Death of Alexander

- Alexander falls ill in Babylon and dies after several days of fever at the age of 32. His sudden death leaves his empire without a clear heir.

323 BC: Division of the Empire

- After Alexander's death, his empire is divided among his generals, the Diadochi, leading to the formation of several Hellenistic kingdoms: the Ptolemaic Kingdom in Egypt, the Seleucid Empire in Persia and Mesopotamia, and the Antigonid dynasty in Macedonia.

PART 1: ORIGINS OF A CONQUEROR

CHAPTER 1. THE WORLD BEFORE ALEXANDER

Before Alexander the Great carved his empire across three continents, before he marched across deserts and mountains, and before the known world echoed his name in awe, there existed a world already ancient and storied, a patchwork of kingdoms, empires, city-states, and cultures vying for dominance in the eastern Mediterranean and Near East. Alexander was not born into a vacuum. He emerged into a fractured but vibrant stage, shaped by centuries of war, myth, and ambition.

To understand Alexander's meteoric rise and unprecedented conquest, we must first understand the world he inherited: the declining unity of Greece, the overstretched grandeur of Persia, the fading splendor of Egypt, and the emergence of a once-backward kingdom, Macedon, that would become the crucible of empire.

The Ancient Greek World: Fractured Glory

In the fifth and early fourth centuries BC, the Greek world was both brilliant and broken. The city-states, or poleis, of the Greek mainland and Aegean islands had created a culture of art, philosophy, and political experimentation unmatched in the ancient world. But they were also fiercely independent, proud, and constantly at odds with one another.

The Glory of the Polis

Each polis was a city and a state unto itself, Athens, Sparta, Corinth, Thebes, each with its own government, army, and identity. Collectively, the Greeks referred to themselves as Hellenes, and shared a language, religion, and mythology. They worshipped the Olympian gods, celebrated the Olympic Games, and revered poets like Homer. But despite these shared bonds, unity was elusive.

At the heart of Greek political life was freedom and rivalry. The Athenians pioneered democracy, giving political voice to male citizens. Sparta, by contrast, was a militaristic oligarchy. Thebes alternated between aristocracy and populism. These ideological differences, and their perpetual jockeying for influence, led to war.

The Aftermath of the Peloponnesian War

From 431 to 404 BC, Greece was consumed by the Peloponnesian War, a brutal conflict between the Athenian Empire and the Peloponnesian League, led by Sparta. The war devastated the Greek world. Cities were razed, populations displaced, and economies shattered. When Sparta emerged victorious, it proved incapable of ruling Greece as a unified power.

In the decades that followed, Thebes rose to prominence, only to fall. Athens regained cultural power but not empire. A pattern of short-lived alliances, betrayals, and wars defined Greek politics. By the time of Alexander's birth in 356 BC, the Greek world was exhausted, fragmented, and vulnerable, ripe for a new power to assert dominance.

The Persian Empire: A Fading Colossus

To the east loomed Persia, the greatest empire the world had yet seen. Founded by Cyrus the Great in the sixth century BC, the Achaemenid Empire had stretched from the Aegean Sea to the Indus River, encompassing Egypt, Mesopotamia, Anatolia, and Central Asia. Its rulers had been called King of Kings, its wealth legendary, its bureaucracy vast.

By Alexander's era, however, Persia was a colossus with cracked foundations.

The Glory Days of Persia

Under rulers like Darius I and Xerxes I, the Persian Empire built monumental cities, Persepolis, Susa, Babylon, and pioneered advanced systems of roads, communication, and governance. The Royal Road linked the empire from west to east, and the use of satraps (provincial governors) allowed for efficient control over vast territories. Persia tolerated local customs and religions, which helped maintain relative peace among diverse peoples.

But its greatest glory came with its greatest humiliation.

The Persian Wars

Between 490 and 479 BC, the Persian kings attempted to conquer Greece. Their campaigns were disastrous. The battles of Marathon, Thermopylae, Salamis, and Plataea became legendary tales of Greek resistance. Though small, divided, and outnumbered, the Greeks repelled the Persian invasions and preserved their independence. These events had a profound psychological impact on both worlds.

To the Greeks, the Persian Empire was a barbaric despotism, powerful but decadent, rich but soft. To the Persians, the Greeks were rebellious irritants, constantly stirring trouble on the western frontier. This legacy of enmity and disdain would shape the ambitions of Alexander, who grew up steeped in stories of Greek heroism against Persian tyranny.

Decline and Instability

By the mid-fourth century BC, Persia was plagued by internal strife, weak leadership, and court intrigue. King Artaxerxes III had tried to restore stability but was poisoned. His successors were increasingly ineffectual or unpopular. When Darius III rose to power in 336 BC, the empire's prestige was waning. Though still enormous, Persia had become bureaucratically bloated, militarily sluggish, and politically brittle.

It remained rich, immeasurably so, but riches alone could not stop what was coming.

Egypt and the Near East: Between Empires

Southwest of Persia lay Egypt, a once-mighty civilization now under Persian control. By the fourth century BC, Egypt had experienced nearly 2,000 years of greatness, including the pyramids, pharaonic dynasties, and religious innovations that had awed the ancient world.

But its independence had been broken. After being conquered by Cambyses II in 525 BC, Egypt passed in and out of Persian hands. By the time of Alexander, the Egyptians resented Persian rule. They clung to their traditions but had become a province of empire, waiting for a liberator.

To the northeast lay the remnants of the Assyrian and Babylonian empires. Once dominant, these regions had been subsumed by Persia. Cities like Nineveh and Babylon retained cultural importance but lacked political independence.

The Near East, then, was a patchwork of proud but conquered peoples, Chaldeans, Arameans, Phoenicians, each with ancient traditions, but all living under the Persian yoke. They too, like the Greeks, might welcome a conqueror who promised change.

The Rise of Macedon: A New Power from the North

Amid this landscape of fractured city-states and overstretched empires, a new force stirred in the north, Macedon, a rugged kingdom long dismissed by the Greeks as semi-barbarian. Yet it was Macedon, under the leadership of one brilliant man, Philip II, that would reshape the political map of the ancient world and set the stage for his son's even greater exploits.

A Kingdom on the Margins

Macedon was geographically and culturally distinct. Located north of classical Greece, bordered by Illyria and Thrace, it was a land of mountains, forests, and horse-breeding plains. Its people spoke a dialect of Greek but were viewed by the southerners as rough and unsophisticated.

Politically, Macedon had been a weak and fragmented monarchy for centuries, vulnerable to invasions and tribal revolts. Its nobility was powerful, its succession uncertain, and its army undisciplined.

But all of that began to change in 359 BC.

Philip II: The Architect of Empire

When Philip II became king, Macedon was on the brink of collapse. His brother had died in battle. Enemies encircled the kingdom. But Philip was no ordinary monarch, he was one of the most brilliant political and military minds of his age. While held hostage in Thebes during his youth, he had learned Greek military tactics and politics firsthand. On returning to Macedon, he set about reforming everything.

- He reorganized the army into a professional, full-time force.

- He introduced the sarissa, a long spear that gave the Macedonian phalanx a devastating advantage.

- He created a corps of elite cavalry and drilled his forces relentlessly.

- He used diplomacy, bribery, marriage, and war to secure Macedon's borders and extend its influence.

Philip II of Macedon

Within a decade, Philip had transformed Macedon from a marginal kingdom into the most powerful state in the Greek world. He intervened in southern Greek politics, subdued rebellious city-states, and founded the League of Corinth, uniting the Greeks under his leadership, willingly or not.

Preparing for Persia

Philip's ultimate goal was to lead a Pan-Hellenic campaign against Persia, to avenge the invasions of the previous century and to seize the riches of the East. In 336 BC, as he prepared his army for this grand enterprise, he was assassinated, stabbed during the wedding celebrations of his daughter in Aegae.

The assassin was Pausanias, a member of Philip's bodyguard, but questions lingered - had Olympias, Philip's fourth wife, orchestrated it to secure the throne for her son?

In the chaos that followed, it was a young man of twenty, Alexander, who seized power.

The State of the World into Which Alexander Was Born

Alexander was born in 356 BC, in the royal palace of Pella, the capital of Macedon. His father, Philip II, was at the height of his early conquests. His mother, Olympias, was a princess from Epirus, a fierce and ambitious woman who claimed descent from Achilles.

From birth, Alexander was raised with the belief that he was destined for greatness. He was told he was a descendant of heroes and gods. According to legend, on the night of his birth, the Temple of Artemis at Ephesus burned, a sign that something world-changing had occurred.

His tutors would include the philosopher Aristotle, who taught him not only logic and science but also a love for Homer, history, and destiny. Alexander devoured stories of Achilles, Heracles, and Cyrus. From a young age, he imagined himself among them.

But the world he inherited was no fantasy. It was fragmented, violent, and volatile.

- Greece was weary of war yet bristling with pride and independence.

- Persia was still powerful, but vulnerable.

- Egypt and the Near East were ancient cultures under foreign rule.

- Macedon, under Philip, was rising, but its future remained uncertain.

In this landscape of shifting power and growing possibility, a new kind of conqueror was about to emerge.

CHAPTER 2. CHILDHOOD AND EDUCATION

The Palace at Pella

Alexander's early years unfolded within the sprawling palace complex of Pella, a city situated in northern Greece, near the Thermaic Gulf. Though Macedon had long been dismissed by southern Greeks as rustic and backward, Pella was a seat of rising power and cosmopolitan wealth. Artisans, merchants, and soldiers moved through its courtyards. Ambassadors came from Athens, Thebes, and Thrace. The palace itself housed libraries, training grounds, banquet halls, and temples.

Within these marble corridors and painted chambers, Alexander absorbed both the chaos and grandeur of court life. He saw his father govern, plot, and campaign. He heard rumors of assassinations, marriages of alliance, and wars of expansion. Macedonian politics were as violent as they were vibrant, and the young prince grew up in a world where power was seized, not inherited.

Even in infancy, he was surrounded by warriors, philosophers, and foreign guests. At a time when most children in the ancient world were taught to survive, Alexander was taught to command.

The Fire of Olympias

If Philip was the architect of Macedonian power, Olympias was the fire that forged Alexander's spirit.

Born a princess of Epirus, Olympias claimed descent from Achilles, and her homeland took pride in its ancient heroic traditions. She brought with her to Macedon a fierce pride, a devotion to religion, especially to the cults of Dionysus and the snake-goddess, and an unyielding belief in her son's destiny.

Olympias of Macedonia by Desiderio da Settignano

Olympias was not content to be a passive consort. She was fiercely protective of Alexander's inheritance and deeply resentful of Philip's other wives and children. The Macedonian court was often divided between those loyal to Olympias and those aligned with other factions.

She whispered to Alexander of his divine origins. Some claimed she told him his true father was not Philip, but Zeus, and that lightning had struck her womb the night of his conception. Whether literal or allegorical, the effect was profound. Alexander grew up believing in his own myth.

She also introduced him to mysterious religious and ecstatic rituals, imbuing him with a fascination for the divine, the prophetic, and the symbolic. Where Philip taught strategy and power, Olympias gave Alexander his sense of purpose, not just to rule, but to transcend mortality.

The Discipline of Philip

Where Olympias was fire, Philip II was steel. A veteran of war and politics, Philip had turned Macedon from a vulnerable border state into the dominant power in Greece. He was brilliant, ruthless, and endlessly pragmatic. Though often absent on campaign, he took a deep interest in his son's upbringing.

Philip understood that greatness was not inherited, it had to be forged. He surrounded Alexander with the best tutors, exposed him to court debates, and encouraged him to observe military reviews and councils. From a young age, Alexander watched generals plot invasions and listened to arguments on alliances and treaties.

Philip also gave his son a model of kingship, not merely by instruction, but by example. He showed how to win loyalty, how to use both fear and generosity, how to play allies against enemies. He was charismatic, physically imposing, and almost always victorious. For Alexander, this was both inspiration and competition.

The father and son had a complex relationship. Philip respected Alexander's intelligence and promise, but also saw in him the defiance of Olympias. Alexander, for his part, admired Philip's accomplishments but often bristled at his father's infidelities and political maneuvering. As Philip remarried, most fatefully to Cleopatra Eurydice, a Macedonian noblewoman, Alexander began to fear for his position as heir.

In many ways, Alexander's drive to surpass his father became one of the central motivations of his life. 'My father will leave me nothing to conquer' he once lamented. It was not said in jest.

Early Education and Heroic Models

From the age of seven, Alexander was given a structured education by private tutors. These early teachers instructed him in reading, writing, music, horsemanship, and martial training. Macedonian boys of the nobility were expected to be both literate and deadly, cultured and courageous.

But even in childhood, Alexander was not like other boys.

He was obsessed with Homer, particularly the Iliad. He saw in Achilles not just a hero, but a spiritual ancestor. He carried a copy of the Iliad annotated by Aristotle into battle. He idolized Heracles, the demigod whose labors conquered monsters and men alike. He read about Cyrus the Great, the Persian founder who had united East and West.

His companions at court included Hephaestion, who would become his lifelong confidant, and other nobles' sons who later became his generals. These boys trained together in weapons and tactics, but Alexander quickly emerged as their leader, brilliant, intense, and destined for command.

A pivotal moment came when he tamed the wild stallion Bucephalus, one of the most famous horses in history, a black horse that none of the other grooms could ride. Observing that the horse was afraid of its own shadow, Alexander turned him to face the sun and rode him effortlessly. Philip was so impressed that he reportedly said, 'My son, seek a kingdom equal to your greatness, Macedon is too small for you.' Alexander named the horse Bucephalus, meaning ox-headed.

That horse would carry Alexander across Asia, and die in India, honored with a city bearing its name.

Bronze coin from Macedonia, minted under the Roman emperor Severus Alexander (222-235), with head of Alexander the Great and young Alexander taming Bucephalos.

The Mind of Aristotle

At age thirteen, Alexander's education took a dramatic turn. His father summoned Aristotle, the greatest philosopher of the age, to tutor the prince. Philip reportedly paid the philosopher handsomely, even rebuilding the town of Stageira, Aristotle's birthplace, as part of the agreement.

Under Aristotle's tutelage, Alexander was introduced to philosophy, science, politics, medicine, geography, ethics, and logic. The sessions took place in the quiet retreat of Mieza, away from court intrigue. It was there that Alexander developed his curiosity about the world, his deep appreciation for Greek culture, and his belief in the ordering of human society.

But Aristotle was not merely an academic. He tailored his teachings to suit a future king. He emphasized practical ethics, governance, and leadership. He urged Alexander to seek knowledge but to also understand the nature of power and the duties of a ruler. He instilled in him a belief in Greek superiority, yet also a fascination with the cultures of the East.

Alexander would later carry these lessons into battle and empire. He saw conquest not only as domination, but as the expansion of civilization. He revered learning, patronized scholars, and built cities as centers of culture. Though he and Aristotle would later differ, particularly on Alexander's desire to integrate Persians into Greek governance, the foundation had been laid.

Aristotle helped Alexander see the world not just as a battlefield, but as a stage for ideas.

Forming a Worldview

By his mid-teens, Alexander was already mentally, physically, and politically precocious. He debated with visiting diplomats. He studied maps of Persia and India. He asked questions about foreign lands, mythological beasts, and the causes of the stars.

He also began to see himself not just as a prince, but as a man chosen for a higher purpose.

Thanks to Olympias, he believed in divine descent. Thanks to Philip, he understood the brutal mechanics of power. Thanks to Aristotle, he saw the world as a place to be studied, ruled, and improved.

He grew obsessed with reputation and legacy. 'Immortality through achievement' became a personal credo. He studied Achilles and sought to emulate his glorious deeds, but also to surpass them. He listened to tales of Persian decadence and dreamed of reversing history, of crossing the Hellespont not as a defender of Greece, but as its avenger and champion.

This worldview, shaped in palaces and libraries, in temples and riding grounds, was profoundly expansive. He did not want to rule Macedon. He wanted to reshape the world.

CHAPTER 3. PRINCE TO KING

From Heir to Conqueror

In the summer of 338 BC, the sun set red over the plains of Boeotia, staining the land where Greek freedom died. The Battle of Chaeronea, fought between the Macedonian army of Philip II and a coalition of southern Greek city-states, was not just a military engagement, it was a reckoning. And amid the thunder of hooves and the clash of sarissas, a young prince earned his name in blood.

Alexander was eighteen. Still barely a man, still untested in the ways of power, he led the elite Companion Cavalry into the heart of the enemy line. As the Athenian and Theban forces buckled, it was Alexander's daring charge that struck the decisive blow. Some said he broke the famed Theban Sacred Band himself. Others whispered that he moved like Achilles reborn.

Whatever the truth, one thing was clear: a prince had become a warrior.

But fate would not wait long. Within two years, Alexander would wear the crown of Macedon, not through gradual inheritance, but through fire, blood, and betrayal. At twenty, he would become the master of a kingdom his father had forged, and would soon dream of something even greater.

The Lion at Chaeronea

The Greek world had long resisted unity. Even after decades of Persian threat and internecine war, the city-states still clung to their independence. When Philip of Macedon began asserting dominance over Greece, the southern cities viewed him with suspicion, resentment, and fear. Athens, Thebes, and their allies formed a final coalition to resist him, and so the stage was set at Chaeronea, a dusty plain northwest of Athens.

The Macedonian army was a revolutionary force. It combined the deep phalanx of sarissa-wielding infantry with flexible cavalry units, disciplined archers, and siege engineers. Philip had spent years perfecting its tactics. But at Chaeronea, he entrusted the most dangerous maneuver, not to a veteran general, but to his son.

As the battle raged, Philip feigned retreat on the Macedonian right. The Greeks pursued, overextending themselves. At the critical moment, Alexander, commanding the Macedonian left, led the Companion Cavalry in a ferocious assault that shattered the Theban line. The Sacred Band, long the pride of Greece, stood their ground but were surrounded and annihilated.

It was a massacre, but also a message. The old Greek order was finished.

Philip's victory forced the southern city-states into the League of Corinth, a new alliance with Macedon at its head. He declared himself the hegemon of Greece and began preparations for his great dream: an invasion of the Persian Empire.

At the center of this future stood Alexander, now tested in battle, admired by the army, and known across Greece as a new kind of prince, bold, brilliant, and terrifying.

But destiny would not unfold under Philip's rule.

The Death of a King

In 336 BC, Macedon stood on the threshold of greatness. Philip had united Greece. He had reformed the army. He was organizing a vast campaign to avenge the Persian invasions of a century before. The invasion was to begin in Asia Minor. Troops had already been sent. Victory seemed inevitable.

And then, at the height of his power, Philip was murdered.

The setting was Aegae, the ancient Macedonian capital. Philip had come to celebrate the marriage of his daughter Cleopatra to Alexander of Epirus, Olympias' brother. It was meant to be a day of triumph. Dignitaries from across Greece attended. Statues of the twelve Olympian gods were paraded, with a thirteenth added, for Philip himself. It was a declaration of divine status. The king of Macedon was not just powerful, he was ascending toward immortality.

As Philip entered the theater, unguarded, he was struck down by a bodyguard named Pausanias. The assassin fled but was quickly killed. The court was thrown into chaos. Who had ordered the assassination? Was it revenge? A personal grievance? Or was something more sinister at play?

Rumors spread like wildfire. Some claimed Olympias had orchestrated the murder, fearing Philip's new wife, Cleopatra Eurydice, would produce a rival heir. Others whispered that Alexander himself had a hand in it, or at least turned a blind eye. Whether true or not, the deaths that followed seemed to confirm a plot: Cleopatra Eurydice and her infant were soon executed. Olympias returned to court in triumph.

One man remained untouched, Alexander.

A King at Twenty

The moment Philip fell, the fate of Macedon hung in the balance. The empire he had built in Greece was only held together by force and charisma. The Macedonian nobility was powerful, the army deeply loyal to Philip, and the Greek cities ever ready to rebel. Alexander's claim to the throne was not secure. He was just twenty, surrounded by seasoned generals, dangerous rivals, and uncertain allies.

But Alexander acted with breathtaking speed.

Within days, he secured the loyalty of the army. He stood before them in full armor, invoking his father's legacy and his own role at Chaeronea. The soldiers acclaimed him as king, Alexander III of Macedon. He then moved quickly to neutralize internal threats. Several potential rivals, some of them half-brothers, were killed. Others were exiled. Olympias, always politically ruthless, ensured that any claimants from Philip's other wives were silenced.

Alexander had seized power not by birthright alone, but by audacity.

He then turned to Greece, where the news of Philip's death had unleashed a storm.

A Fragile Empire

Across the Aegean, Greek city-states saw Philip's death as an opportunity to throw off Macedonian domination. In Athens, the orator Demosthenes celebrated the king's assassination and pushed for renewed resistance. In Thebes, rumors of Macedon's weakness led to open talk of revolt. Even in Thessaly and Thrace, distant satraps and tribes began testing Macedonian authority.

Alexander understood that if he hesitated, the entire empire would collapse.

He marched south with terrifying speed. Within weeks, he had reached Thessaly, where he secured the region through negotiation and display of strength. He then continued to Thermopylae, the gateway to central Greece. The city-states, stunned by his boldness and the presence of a fully mobilized Macedonian army, began to capitulate.

At the League of Corinth, Alexander was confirmed as hegemon, just as his father had been. Only Thebes held out.

The Fall of Thebes

Thebes had long been a proud and powerful city, an archrival of Athens and a former ally of Macedon. But with Philip dead and rumors swirling that Alexander had perished in the north, the Thebans rose in revolt. They expelled the Macedonian garrison and prepared for war.

It was a fatal miscalculation.

In the autumn of 335 BC, Alexander marched on Thebes with a vengeance. He offered lenient terms: surrender, and the city would be spared. But the Thebans, still believing they had Greek support, rejected the offer and fortified their walls.

What followed was swift and brutal.

Alexander's forces stormed the city. The resistance was fierce but hopeless. Macedonian siege engineers battered the gates. Infantry poured in. House by house, the city was taken. When the fighting ended, over 6,000 Thebans lay dead. Another 30,000 were sold into slavery. The city was razed, its walls leveled, its legacy erased in a single, apocalyptic moment.

Only temples and the house of the poet Pindar were spared.

The message was unmistakable. Macedonian rule was not to be questioned. Rebellion would be met not with compromise, but annihilation.

A Message to the World

The destruction of Thebes shocked the Greek world. Athens, which had flirted with rebellion, now backed away. Sparta, ever proud, remained defiant but isolated. Across the Aegean, Persian satraps watched warily. Alexander had not just secured his throne, he had made a statement: the boy-king was no puppet, no accidental monarch.

He was, in the words of one ambassador, 'the thunderbolt of Macedon.'

Yet Alexander was not cruel without calculation. After the sack of Thebes, he wrote to the other city-states, declaring that he had punished a traitorous city, not the Greek world as a whole. He forgave Athens, rebuilt alliances, and confirmed treaties. He understood the balance between fear and favor.

He also used religion and culture as tools of legitimacy. At Delphi, he consulted the Oracle. At Olympia, he sponsored athletic games. At Corinth, he was recognized as commander-in-chief of the campaign against Persia, the same role Philip had claimed. It was both a personal and symbolic victory.

By early 334 BC, just a year after Philip's assassination, Alexander had secured his kingdom, reasserted dominance over Greece, and prepared his army for the next step.

The time had come to cross the Hellespont.

The Young King Reimagined

In the span of two years, Alexander had crossed his first great threshold. The Alexander who stood at the helm of Macedon in 334 BC was no longer a youthful prince. He was a king forged in fire, by the blood of Chaeronea, the betrayal at Aegae, and the burning of Thebes. He had weathered palace intrigue, revolts, and foreign threats. And he had emerged not only intact, but exalted.

His army worshipped him. His enemies feared him. His court walked a careful line between awe and uncertainty.

More than that, Alexander had begun to shape his image as a hero and legend. He invoked the gods not only as protectors but as ancestral kin. He positioned himself as the heir of Achilles, the rival of Heracles, the avenger of Greece against Persian tyranny. The world would soon hear his name, not just as a king, but as a force of destiny.

PART II: CONQUEST OF AN EMPIRE

CHAPTER 4. THE PERSIAN CAMPAIGN BEGINS

In the spring of 334 BC, the winds shifted across the Aegean. Ships left the harbor at Sestos, carrying soldiers who had never seen Asia. Banners snapped in the breeze, sunlight flashed off bronze armor, and drums beat time to the oars. At the helm stood a 22-year-old king, watching the receding shores of Europe with fire in his blood. The time for dreaming was over. The time for conquest had begun.

Alexander the Great was crossing the Hellespont, the narrow strait between Europe and Asia, with an army of fewer than 50,000 men. Opposing him was the Persian Empire, still the largest and richest realm the world had ever known, spanning from the Mediterranean to the Hindu Kush. It had ruled for two centuries, absorbed countless civilizations, and defeated armies far larger than Alexander's.

And yet, as the Macedonian fleet touched the Asian shore, it was not the Persians who held the initiative. Alexander did. The young king had inherited more than a throne, he had inherited a mission: to avenge the past, to claim the future, and to burn his name into eternity.

Crossing the Hellespont

The crossing of the Hellespont was more than a logistical feat, it was an act of symbolism, legend, and destiny. Alexander wasn't simply leading an army from Europe to Asia; he was reenacting the path of myth.

According to ancient accounts, Alexander sailed from Sestos to Abydos, the same strait that Xerxes I had once bridged with a massive pontoon crossing during the Persian invasion of Greece 150 years earlier. But where Xerxes had crossed with the aim of subjugating Greece, Alexander now crossed as the avenger, the challenger, the new Achilles.

As his ship neared the Asian coast, Alexander reportedly cast a spear from the bow into the sand, claiming Asia as 'a land won by the spear', an ancient gesture of conquest. When he stepped ashore, he knelt and offered sacrifices to Poseidon, to

Athena, and to Zeus. His mind was never far from the gods, or from the myths he meant to embody.

He also made a pilgrimage to the nearby city of Troy, visiting the tomb of Achilles. There, in full armor, he honored the legendary hero whose story he had memorized since childhood. Some say he ran a race naked around the tomb, as was the Greek tradition for honoring the dead. Others claim he took a shield from the temple to carry into battle.

Whether fact or embellishment, the message was clear: Alexander had come not as a mere general, but as a living myth, striding across history to fulfill a divine purpose.

The Persian Opposition

The Persian Empire, vast as it was, was not ready. Darius III, newly on the throne after a bloody succession struggle, underestimated the scale of the threat. He entrusted the defense of Asia Minor to local satraps (governors) and a force of mercenaries, many of them Greek. While Persian command structures were sophisticated, they were often decentralized and sluggish to react.

Darius III from the Alexander Mosaic, 100 BC, a Roman floor mosaic from Pompeii.

At the heart of Persian weakness was a mistaken belief: that Alexander's campaign was just a northern raid, another Greek nuisance to be suppressed, not the opening salvo of a world-changing war.

The Persian forces stationed in western Anatolia were led by Memnon of Rhodes, a seasoned Greek mercenary commander in Persian service. He advised a strategy of scorched earth, proposing to deny Alexander supplies and lure him inland. But the Persian satraps, proud and divided, rejected the plan. They wanted to crush the invaders in battle, and they chose to make their stand at the Granicus River.

The Battle of the Granicus (May 334 BC)

The Granicus River was not a wide stream, but it was steep-banked, fast-flowing, and flanked by hills. When Alexander's scouts located the Persian forces arrayed on the far side of the riverbank, there was debate in his camp. Some urged caution. It was late in the day. Crossing under enemy fire was risky.

But Alexander had not come to Asia to hesitate.

He gave orders to prepare for an immediate assault.

The Macedonian Army

Alexander's force was compact, professional, and brilliantly organized. It numbered roughly 32,000 infantry and 5,000 cavalry, with a core of Macedonian phalanx soldiers armed with the sarissa, a pike twice the length of the traditional Greek spear. Alongside them were hypaspists (elite infantry), Companion Cavalry (aristocratic horsemen), and allied contingents from Thessaly, Thrace, and other Greek states.

This army was smaller than what Persia could field, but it was unified, loyal, and under a single command. Alexander's presence electrified his men. He shared their hardships, led from the front, and promised glory beyond imagining.

The Persian Forces

On the far bank, the Persians had an army of around 20,000 cavalry and 20,000 Greek mercenary infantry, the latter stationed at the rear. Their plan was to prevent a river crossing, kill Alexander in the chaos, and end the invasion in a single blow.

Memnon's Greek mercenaries were experienced and disciplined, but they were positioned too far back to affect the initial engagement. The front lines were held by Persian nobles and cavalry, who formed a wall along the riverbank.

The Assault

Alexander formed his cavalry into a wedge and personally led the charge into the river.

The river's current pushed against the advancing Macedonians, and the steep bank forced them to climb under a hail of arrows and javelins. The Persian cavalry counterattacked as the Macedonians struggled ashore. The fighting was savage and chaotic.

Alexander was at the center of it all. He wore a white-plumed helmet and fought with spear and sword. He was nearly killed when a Persian noble raised a scimitar to strike him down, but Cleitus the Black, one of his officers, severed the man's arm before the blow landed.

As more Macedonian cavalry gained the bank, they fanned out and created room for the infantry to cross. The phalanx began to deploy. With pressure mounting, the Persian cavalry line broke.

Alexander then turned his attention to the Greek mercenaries, who had been ordered to hold their ground. Surrounded, outflanked, and betrayed by their own commanders' caution, they were slaughtered. Over 18,000 were killed, with a few thousand taken prisoner and sent in chains back to Greece, to toil as slaves in Macedon's mines, a warning to other Greeks who might serve Persia.

The battle was over. Alexander had won his first major engagement on Asian soil.

A King of the Greeks, and Asia

The victory at Granicus was more than tactical, it was psychological and strategic. It shattered the myth of Persian invincibility and opened the gates of western Anatolia.

Alexander treated the fallen Persian nobles with honor, sending their weapons and armor back to Athens as offerings at the Parthenon. He wrote personally to the Greek city-states, reminding them that he was fighting for Greece, to avenge the past and liberate their fellow Hellenes in Asia.

To his army, he awarded golden wreaths and paid generous bonuses. He knew that morale would win future battles as much as strategy.

To the cities of Anatolia, he offered clemency, but on his terms.

The Welcome in Western Anatolia

As Alexander moved south and west along the Aegean coast, city after city surrendered or welcomed him as a liberator. The harsh rule of Persian satraps, combined with Alexander's propaganda and generosity, made many Anatolian Greeks switch allegiances willingly.

Sardis

One of the first major cities to capitulate was Sardis, the capital of Lydia. It had once been the seat of Croesus, the fabulously wealthy king of legend. Its Persian governor surrendered without resistance. Alexander treated the city with respect and established a Macedonian garrison to secure it.

Sardis's fall symbolized the end of Persian control over western Anatolia.

Ephesus

In Ephesus, a culturally rich Greek city under Persian domination, Alexander was hailed as a liberator. He restored democratic governance and contributed funds to the Temple of Artemis, which had recently been destroyed by fire.

Here, Alexander was playing both conqueror and benefactor. He knew the value of public symbolism, and few acts spoke louder than repairing a temple to a revered goddess.

Miletus and Halicarnassus

Not all cities welcomed him. At Miletus, Persian forces attempted to resist, but Alexander launched a swift siege and captured the city. At Halicarnassus, he faced his most serious challenge since the Granicus.

There, Memnon of Rhodes had regrouped and fortified the city heavily. Alexander launched an aggressive siege, using battering rams and siege towers. The fighting was brutal and lasted weeks. Fires raged through the city, and progress was slow. But eventually, Memnon fled, and the city fell.

The campaign revealed Alexander's tenacity and tactical flexibility. He was willing to use both hammer and scalpel, force and diplomacy, depending on the city and situation.

A Shifting Momentum

By the end of 334 BC, Alexander had secured western Asia Minor, defeated the Persian satrapal army, and gained control over coastal cities that would supply his advance. He had also taken steps to integrate and administer these newly acquired territories.

- He appointed Macedonian satraps or left existing governors in place if they pledged loyalty.
- He established Greek-style democracies in many cities, winning favor among the populace.
- He ensured supply lines and rest stations were set up for future opera-

tions deeper into Persia.

What had begun as an expedition now looked like the dawn of empire.

The Myth Grows

Alexander's personal myth began to swell. His soldiers saw him not only as a brilliant commander but as favored by the gods. He led from the front, was wounded in battle, shared spoils fairly, and invoked legendary heroes at every turn. In return, he demanded unwavering loyalty.

He told his men they were not just marching into Asia, they were marching into history.

Back in Persia, Darius III finally realized the threat. He began organizing a full imperial response. He would not make the same mistake again. The next battle would not be a local skirmish, but an all-out confrontation between two worlds.

In the grand sweep of Alexander's conquests, the year 334 BC may seem modest. No cities burned like Persepolis, no emperors fled as at Gaugamela. But it was in this year, through the storming of a riverbank, the fall of proud cities, and the march across Anatolia, that Alexander laid the foundation for everything that followed.

He had crossed the Hellespont not as a raider, but as a king. He had fought at the Granicus not to survive, but to announce his arrival. And he had marched through Anatolia not to plunder, but to build, an empire that would fuse East and West.

These were the first steps of a journey that would reshape the world.

And he was just getting started.

CHAPTER 5. DEFEATING DARIUS III

The Collapse of an Empire

In the vast plains of the Near East, two worlds collided, East and West, tradition and ambition, empire and legend. At the heart of that collision stood Darius III, Great King of Persia, heir to Cyrus, and ruler of the most extensive empire the ancient world had ever known. Facing him was a younger man, lean, sharp-eyed, already crowned by victory: Alexander of Macedon.

The struggle between these two men would shape the destiny of millions. It would stretch from the rivers of Cilicia to the deserts of Mesopotamia, from the palaces of Babylon to the burning rooftops of Persepolis. It would culminate not in peace or surrender, but in the destruction of a world order that had stood for centuries.

The Road to Issus

After his victory at the Granicus in 334 BC, Alexander swept through western Asia Minor. News of Alexander's success alarmed Darius III, a king recently installed after a palace coup. His throne still unstable, Darius could no longer ignore the Macedonian threat. He assembled an army of imperial scale, infantry, cavalry, archers, chariots, drawing from the corners of the empire: Medes, Bactrians, Egyptians, Indians, and Greeks. He would crush this upstart invader and reaffirm the supremacy of Persia.

Darius marched west, expecting to confront Alexander in central Anatolia. But Alexander, ever audacious, had already crossed the Taurus Mountains into Cilicia, catching the Persians off guard. Darius, seeking to cut him off, moved north, unknowingly placing his massive force in a narrow coastal corridor near Issus.

There, hemmed in by sea and mountains, Darius would lose everything.

The Battle of Issus (333 BC)

The Terrain

The battlefield at Issus was a narrow plain wedged between the Amanus Mountains and the Mediterranean Sea, cut by the Pinarus River. Darius had brought perhaps 100,000–200,000 men, including his royal guard, tens of thousands of cavalry, and a vast contingent of infantry.

But in the tight confines of the plain, Darius could not deploy his full force. His numbers became a disadvantage, his men crammed together, their flanks vulnerable. Alexander, with around 40,000 troops, immediately saw the opportunity.

Alexander and Bucephalus, Battle of Issus mosaic

The Strategy

Alexander placed his phalanx at the center, Thessalian and allied cavalry on the left, and his elite Companion Cavalry with hypaspists on the right, shield-bearers and his traditional strike wing, which he personally led.

At the battle's onset, Alexander charged across the river on the right, smashing into the Persian left flank. His cavalry punched through, driving back enemy horsemen and attacking the Persian center from the side.

Darius, positioned at the heart of his army in a golden chariot, watched in growing panic as his flank collapsed. Macedonian infantry, after fierce resistance, broke through the Persian line. Alexander aimed straight for Darius.

The Flight of the King

As Macedonian spears closed in, Darius lost his nerve. He turned his chariot around and fled the field, abandoning his army, his royal standard, his bow, and even his family. His retreat triggered panic. The Persian line broke. Thousands were cut down as they tried to flee. The royal camp was overrun.

Darius' driver whipping his horses and the Persian army retreats

Alexander's army had achieved the impossible: defeating the King of Kings in open battle and sent him fleeing into the east.

Among the spoils were Darius's wife, daughters, and mother, who were treated with great dignity by Alexander. He would later marry one of the daughters, Statira, cementing his claim to the Persian throne.

Issus was not only a military triumph; it was a symbolic deathblow. The Persian Empire had cracked, and Alexander's legend was now unassailable.

March Toward the Heartland

Following Issus, Alexander marched south, down the Levantine coast. He was methodical, cutting off Persian naval bases and capturing or besieging cities.

Siege of Tyre

The most dramatic of these was the Siege of Tyre, a heavily fortified island city half a mile off the Phoenician coast. When Tyre refused to allow Alexander entry, he responded with a seven-month siege.

To reach the city, Alexander ordered the construction of a massive causeway (or mole) stretching from the mainland to the island. Tyrians fiercely resisted, launching attacks by ship and raining projectiles on workers. The siege dragged on for seven grueling months, with Alexander employing siege towers, battering rams, and naval reinforcements from conquered Phoenician cities.

Alexander the Great at the Siege of Tyre

Eventually, the causeway reached the walls, and Alexander's forces breached them with a two-pronged assault—from both land and sea. The city fell in July 332 BCE. In retribution for the stubborn resistance, Alexander executed about 2,000 defenders and sold thousands more into slavery, though he spared those who had taken refuge in temples.

The Destruction of Gaza

Following his conquest of Tyre, Alexander marched south toward Egypt. On the way, he encountered fierce resistance from Gaza, a heavily fortified city strategically located on the coastal route between Egypt and the Levant.

In late 332 BCE, the Persian-appointed governor of Gaza, Batis, refused to surrender. Gaza sat atop a high hill and was reinforced with strong defenses. Alexander launched a siege that lasted two months, using siege towers and battering rams to breach the walls. The defenders resisted fiercely, and Alexander himself was wounded during the assault.

When Gaza finally fell, Alexander enacted a brutal punishment. Batis was captured alive, but Alexander, enraged by the prolonged resistance, ordered him executed in a particularly cruel fashion: Batis was tied by his heels to a chariot and dragged around the city, echoing Achilles' treatment of Hector in the Iliad. The city was sacked, and its male population killed or enslaved.

The message at Tyre and Gaza was brutal but effective: resistance to Alexander would not be tolerated.

Alexander then marched into Egypt, where he was welcomed as a liberator. The Egyptians, resentful of Persian rule, offered little resistance. He founded Alexandria and was crowned pharaoh, as we will see in the next chapter.

But his ultimate prize still lay ahead, Darius, and the heart of the Persian Empire.

The Battle of Gaugamela (331 BC)

Darius had regrouped. He now assembled an even larger force, possibly 250,000 or more, though ancient sources likely exaggerated. This time, he chose his ground carefully: the plain of Gaugamela, near Arbela (modern Erbil, Iraq), around 700 miles northeast of Gaza.

The battlefield was flattened by engineers to maximize the effectiveness of scythed chariots and cavalry. Darius had elephants, thousands of archers, elite cavalry, and once again took the field in person.

Alexander had 47,000 men.

The Night Before

On the night before the battle, Alexander reportedly slept soundly. When asked why, he replied, 'Because I am not marching against a hidden enemy, but against a known one.'

His confidence was supreme. His men trusted him. The next day would decide the fate of Asia.

The Battle

Darius placed cavalry on both flanks, with scythed chariots at the front. Alexander again anchored his left with Thessalian cavalry, and his right with the Companions, which he led.

As the Persian cavalry attacked, Alexander shifted his phalanx diagonally, drawing Darius's forces to the flanks. He then identified a gap in the Persian center, left open by overextension, and charged straight at Darius.

Once more, panic rippled through the Persian ranks. Darius fled. The center collapsed. Persian morale shattered. Thousands were slain, and the road to Babylon was open.

The Fall of Babylon, Susa, and Persepolis

After Gaugamela, the Persian world began to unravel.

Babylon

The majestic city of Babylon, seat of Mesopotamian culture for millennia, opened its gates without resistance. The satrap Mazaeus surrendered the city and was retained by Alexander as governor, a clever blend of conquest and continuity.

Alexander entered the city in triumph. He sacrificed to Babylonian gods, honored local traditions, and released prisoners. His strategy was clear: to rule not just through arms, but through assimilation.

Susa

Next came Susa, another ancient capital. It too surrendered peacefully. Here Alexander seized a vast treasure, 50,000 talents of silver, enough to pay his troops and finance future campaigns. He sent part of the wealth back to Macedon, reinforcing his legitimacy at home.

In Susa, Alexander took symbolic control of the imperial regalia, robes, crowns, and artifacts that once belonged to Cyrus and Darius.

Persepolis: The Heart of Persia

Finally, Alexander marched on Persepolis, the ceremonial capital of the Achaemenid dynasty. Situated in the mountains of Persis, it was a city of stone and gold, of colossal palaces and fluted columns. Built by Darius I and Xerxes, it represented the spiritual and imperial heart of Persia.

Alexander entered the city in early 330 BC, after its defenders retreated. The city surrendered, but the legacy it carried could not be so easily subdued.

The Destruction of Persepolis

At first, Alexander treated Persepolis with reverence. But over the following weeks, something changed. Whether through drunken fury, calculation, or divine retribution, Alexander made a fateful decision.

One night, after a banquet, possibly encouraged by a courtesan named Thaïs, Alexander ordered the palace of Xerxes to be burned.

Torches were thrown. Flames consumed the cedar roofs, licked up the walls, and melted gold. The fire raged for days. Ancient murals, sculptures, scrolls, and symbols of empire were turned to ash.

Why did he do it?

Some believed it was revenge, a symbolic retaliation for Xerxes' burning of Athens 150 years earlier. Others saw it as a calculated act, a declaration that the old Persian world was dead, and that a new world, his world, had begun.

Alexander reportedly regretted the act the next morning, walking through the ruins in silence. But the message had been sent.

Persepolis, once the jewel of Asia, now smoldered in ruins.

Darius's Last Stand and Death

Even after Gaugamela, Darius III had not surrendered. He fled eastward, attempting to rally resistance. Alexander pursued, determined to capture the Great King alive. But Darius's own nobles, including Bessus, a Bactrian satrap, realizing the futility of resistance, betrayed and assassinated him in 330 BC, leaving his body in the road for Alexander to find.

When Alexander came upon the dying Darius, he wept. He ordered the assassins to be hunted down and executed. He gave Darius a royal funeral, buried him with honor, and declared himself the true heir to the Achaemenid line.

In Persian eyes, Alexander was no longer an invader, he had become Shahanshah, the King of Kings.

The Fall of an Empire

The defeat of Darius III was more than a victory over a man, it was the extinction of a world. In just three years, Alexander had shattered an empire that had ruled for centuries, crushed armies ten times his size, and walked triumphantly through the capitals of Babylon, Susa, and Persepolis.

But his conquest was more than military. He had absorbed Persia, its titles, customs, and vision of rule. He wore Persian robes, adopted Persian court etiquette, and began to forge a new identity, not simply as a Greek conqueror, but as the fusion of East and West.

Yet the destruction of Persepolis remained a lingering paradox. It was the moment of his greatest power, and perhaps the first shadow of the contradictions that would define the rest of his reign.

From the flaming ruins of Persepolis, Alexander would march further east, toward new enemies, new dreams, and the edge of the known world.

But he had already changed history. The old empires had fallen. The age of Alexander had begun.

CHAPTER 6. INTO EGYPT

Liberator, Pharaoh, and Son of Zeus

The Nile shimmered under the desert sun as Alexander of Macedon crossed into Egypt in the late autumn of 332 BC. He did not come as a conqueror drenched in fire and blood, as he had in Asia Minor or Mesopotamia. He came as something far rarer, a liberator.

For two centuries, Egypt had been under the heel of the Persian Empire. It had been ruled by foreign satraps, taxed, and drained of its autonomy. Its people, proud heirs of one of the world's oldest civilizations, had chafed under Achaemenid rule. When Alexander entered the land of the Nile, not a single arrow was loosed in defense of the Persian overlords.

Instead, the gates of Egypt opened. The priests welcomed him. The people celebrated. The Persian satrap fled. And in a remarkable twist of fate, this young Macedonian king, just 24 years old, was hailed as the new Pharaoh of Egypt, the living link between heaven and earth.

But for Alexander, Egypt was more than a strategic province. It was a stage for mythmaking, a theater in which he could fuse conquest with divinity, politics with immortality.

And so, he began one of the most extraordinary chapters of his campaign, not one of war, but of vision, city-building, and divine revelation.

Welcomed as a Liberator

After his brutal siege and sack of Tyre, and the dramatic occupation of Gaza, Alexander moved steadily toward Egypt. The Persians had stationed a satrap there, Mazaces, but his forces were meager. When news reached him of Tyre's fall and Gaza's destruction, he made the only rational choice: surrender.

In contrast to the resistance he had faced in Phoenicia, Egypt offered no battle. It offered praise.

As Alexander marched into Memphis, the ancient capital of Lower Egypt, he was greeted not as an invader but as a redeemer. Priests of the temples approached him in processions. Bulls were sacrificed. Hymns were sung in his honor. Crowds lined the streets to witness the arrival of the man who had broken Persian chains.

In a land where kings were gods, symbolism mattered, and Alexander understood it better than any conqueror before or after. He performed the necessary rituals at the great temple of Ptah, offered sacrifices to Apis, the sacred bull of fertility and kingship, and was formally crowned by the Egyptian priesthood.

To the Egyptians, this coronation was not political theater. In their eyes, Alexander was now the son of Ra, the divine ruler who maintained order in the cosmos. His name was inscribed in hieroglyphs as Pharaoh, nestled in a royal cartouche, the ancient symbol of kingship.

Thus began the transformation of Alexander the warrior into Alexander the god-king.

The Founding of Alexandria

Yet Alexander was not content to merely rule Egypt; he would reshape it. From the moment he arrived, his strategic and visionary mind turned to the coast.

To the west of the Nile Delta lay a stretch of land between the Mediterranean Sea and a brackish lake called Mareotis. It was well-situated, close to the Nile for agricultural access, open to the sea for trade, and flanked by the island of Pharos, a natural harbor.

There, Alexander decided, he would build a city worthy of legend.

A City by Divine Will

According to tradition, Alexander personally marked out the plan of the new city in the sand with flour, tracing walls, boulevards, and marketplaces. His architects, including the famed Dinocrates, advised on the structure: a grid layout, wide streets, separate quarters for Greeks, Egyptians, and foreigners, and a massive causeway connecting the island of Pharos to the mainland.

When birds swooped down and ate the flour, Alexander's companions took it as a bad omen. But he countered that it meant the city would feed the world, a prophetic vision that would later prove true.

He named the city Alexandria, the first of more than twenty that would bear his name, but destined to become the greatest.

Future of the City

Though Alexander would never see the city finished, Alexandria would become the intellectual, economic, and cultural center of the ancient world.

- It would house the Great Library, repository of hundreds of thousands of scrolls and the dream of universal knowledge.

- It would host the Museum, a scholarly institution unlike any other, drawing thinkers from Greece, Egypt, India, and beyond.

- It would thrive as a port of trade, linking Africa, Asia, and Europe in a way no city ever had before.

Alexander's name became synonymous with cosmopolitan civilization, a monument in stone and scholarship that endured far longer than any battlefield.

The Lighthouse of Alexandria by Magdalena van de Pasee, one of the 7 Wonders of the Ancient World

Son of Zeus-Ammon

For Alexander, Egypt was not merely a territory to be administered or a people to be ruled. It was a place of mystery, prophecy, and divine affirmation.

In early 331 BC, he set out across the Western Desert toward a distant, sacred oasis: Siwa.

The Journey to Siwa

It was a journey filled with danger. The route to the Oracle of Ammon crossed hundreds of miles of barren wilderness, where shifting sands, mirages, and dehydration threatened every step. According to legend, the party became lost until two ravens guided them to safety, seen as a sign from the gods.

Some ancient sources speak of sudden rainstorms sent to relieve the column, or of mysterious serpents lighting the way. These stories, likely apocryphal, still reflect the mystical atmosphere that surrounded the journey.

For Alexander, reaching Siwa was not about convenience. It was a pilgrimage, a quest for divine identity.

The Oracle of Ammon

The Oracle of Zeus-Ammon at Siwa was one of the most respected in the ancient world, blending Greek and Egyptian religious traditions. Ammon was portrayed as a ram-headed deity, associated with the Egyptian god Amun and the Greek Zeus.

When Alexander entered the temple, the priests led him in alone. What was said has remained a secret of history, but ancient writers have suggested that the oracle addressed Alexander as the son of Zeus, confirming what he had long believed: that he was no mere man, but divinely born.

Some say the priest greeted him with, 'O son of Zeus, what do you seek?' Others suggest that Alexander asked whether all of Philip's murderers had been punished, and whether he would rule the world.

The answers, if they were real, were affirmative.

Upon exiting the temple, Alexander's demeanor had changed. He spoke less of mortals and more of fate. He wrote to his mother, Olympias, but addressed her not as 'mother' but as one favored by the gods.

The transformation was complete. Alexander had gone into the desert as a king and returned as a demigod.

Consolidating Egypt

Having received divine affirmation, Alexander returned to Memphis to consolidate his rule. He established Greek-speaking administrators, left behind garrisons, and ensured the temples and priests were respected. He was careful not to interfere with local traditions.

In doing so, he ensured that Egypt would remain peaceful during his eastern campaigns and long after his death. Unlike many conquerors, Alexander understood that to rule Egypt, one had to be accepted within its spiritual and cultural order.

He appointed a Persian, Cleomenes of Naucratis, to oversee the region, an unusual but strategic decision. Cleomenes, despite later being infamous for greed and corruption, kept order.

Alexander left behind both an empire and a myth, a god-king who walked among pyramids, worshipped Isis and Amun, and understood Egypt not as a land to be conquered, but as a key to immortality.

Departure from Egypt

By the summer of 331 BC, Alexander had spent several peaceful and productive months in Egypt. His rear was secure, his legend expanded, and his army rested. But the great campaign was not over.

As we saw in the previous chapter, he turned his attention eastward, toward Babylon, Susa, and Persepolis, toward Darius III and the very throne of Persia.

Before departing, he made final offerings to the Egyptian gods and received embassies from Greek cities now firmly under his influence. His men, rejuvenated by the interlude in Egypt, were ready to march again.

But even as he left, Alexander had irrevocably changed the land he'd touched.

Egypt would never again be merely a province of empires. For centuries to come, it would carry the memory of a foreigner who became a Pharaoh, who built a city on the sea, and who walked into the desert to hear the voice of a god.

Legacy of Egypt

A Pharaoh Among Pharaohs

Alexander is one of the few foreigners ever accepted as Pharaoh by the Egyptian priesthood. His name appears on temple walls, in hieroglyphic cartouches, among the long line of divine kings. He is shown making offerings to Ra, Osiris, and Isis, his face stylized in the Egyptian artistic tradition.

Though he ruled Egypt for only a few months, his impact echoed for centuries.

Alexandria: A Living Monument

His city would go on to surpass even his dreams. Alexandria became the capital of Ptolemaic Egypt, the site of the Lighthouse of Pharos, one of the Seven Wonders of the Ancient World, and a center of science, philosophy, and multicultural exchange.

Though the man would die far away, his body would eventually be interred in Alexandria, enshrined in a golden sarcophagus, visited by emperors and legends.

To the Egyptians, Alexander was not only a memory. He was a monarch, a deity, and a founder.

PART III. AT THE EDGE OF THE WORLD

CHAPTER 7. ACROSS CENTRAL ASIA

Conquest, Resistance, and Fusion in the East

The burning ruins of Persepolis still smoldered behind him when Alexander turned his gaze eastward. The heartland of the Persian Empire had fallen, Babylon, Susa, Persepolis, yet Alexander's ambition remained unsatisfied. The world was vast, and the limits of it were still undefined in his mind. There were territories beyond the Iranian plateau, in the lands of Bactria and Sogdiana, unsubdued, untamed, and for him, unfinished.

From 330 to 327 BC, Alexander led his army through the highlands and deserts of Central Asia, into regions where Persian control had always been tenuous and local resistance fierce. This was not a swift march of conquest, but a grinding, complex war of attrition. It was a campaign of sieges, ambushes, harsh winters, and insurgencies. But it was also a time of transformation, for Alexander as a ruler, and for the empire he was forging.

It was in these rugged lands that he faced the most stubborn opposition, and also where he made one of his most fateful decisions: the marriage to Roxana, a Bactrian noblewoman who would symbolize his attempt to bind Greek and eastern worlds in a single destiny.

Pursuit of the Shadow King

After the death of Darius III, Alexander assumed not just the role of conqueror, but of legitimate heir to the Persian throne. Bessus, who killed Darius, declared himself King Artaxerxes V, retreated deep into Bactria (roughly modern-day Afghanistan), rallying resistance among local warlords, nomadic tribes, and remnants of Persian authority.

To consolidate his rule, Alexander needed to eliminate Bessus, stamp out resistance in the east, and integrate these frontier regions into his growing empire. But the terrain ahead was unlike anything he had faced before.

Crossing into Bactria in 330 BC, Alexander entered a world of soaring mountains, barren plateaus, and narrow valleys ideal for guerrilla warfare. This was no place for phalanxes to march in unison. Here, Macedonian discipline would clash with guile, speed, and intimate knowledge of the land.

The Bactrian Campaign

Bactria was ruled not by cities but by fortified hill settlements and semi-nomadic clans. After Bessus fled across the Oxus River (modern Amu Darya), Alexander followed with relentless speed, often splitting his forces and moving by night, catching enemies unprepared.

Though Bessus attempted to rally support, his authority was weak and his betrayal of Darius discredited him. Eventually, his own allies, led by Spitamenes, a powerful Sogdian noble, turned against him, hoping to secure favor with Alexander. Bessus was captured, whipped, and sent back for execution, possibly crucified, as a public punishment for regicide.

Alexander now claimed the Persian kingship not by conquest alone, but as avenger and successor. The official regalia of the Great King was his. But the land was far from subdued.

The deeper he went into the east, the more personal and brutal the conflict became.

Sogdiana and the War of Attrition

If Bactria was hard to tame, Sogdiana was a nightmare.

Located north of the Oxus River, Sogdiana was a patchwork of deserts, mountain passes, and fortress towns. It was strategically crucial, serving as a gateway between the Persian heartland and the frontiers of India, but politically fragmented. Here, resistance to Alexander grew fiercer.

The war in Sogdiana evolved into a protracted insurgency, led first by Spitamenes. He was no mere bandit. Spitamenes was a clever and charismatic leader who understood how to exploit the weaknesses of Alexander's lines of communication. He stirred rebellion, led surprise cavalry raids, and ambushed isolated garrisons. He rallied local tribes and used the terrain to his advantage.

Alexander responded with a combination of ruthless reprisals and strategic innovation.

- He burned resistant villages, slaughtered rebels, and deported entire populations.

- He divided his forces into smaller mobile units capable of fast pursuit.

- He built and left behind fortresses and garrisons to secure key routes.

- He founded cities as outposts of order and Hellenic culture.

This was not glory-seeking conquest but methodical empire-building, but it came at a cost. The Macedonians grew exhausted and frustrated. The constant marching, harsh weather, and stubborn resistance wore down morale.

But Alexander refused to retreat. The east would be conquered, not for plunder or prestige, but to complete the dream of a unified empire.

The Siege of the Sogdian Rock

One of the most famous episodes of the Central Asian campaign was the siege of the Sogdian Rock, a natural fortress perched atop a steep cliff, thought to be impregnable. Local nobles had gathered there with their families, thinking themselves safe from the Macedonian advance.

When Alexander demanded their surrender, they mocked him: 'You'll need soldiers with wings to take this place.'

Alexander almost obliged! He summoned his best climbers, 300 volunteers trained for assault, and under the cover of night, they scaled the cliff with ropes and tent pegs hammered into crevices. A few fell to their deaths. But by dawn, the survivors stood atop the ridge above the fortress.

When they showed themselves to the defenders below, it broke their will.

The Sogdian Rock surrendered without a fight. Among those inside was Roxana, the daughter of a local noble named Oxyartes.

What followed was not merely a romantic tale, it was a strategic masterstroke.

The Marriage to Roxana

Roxana was a teenager at the time, described by ancient sources as intelligent, dignified, and beautiful. Alexander, whether moved by love or political calculation, or both, chose to marry her in 327 BC.

The marriage shocked his Macedonian officers, many of whom had expected him to take a Greek or Macedonian bride. But Alexander had a vision larger than dynastic politics.

The marriage of Alexander and Roxana

By wedding a Bactrian noblewoman, Alexander signaled his intent to integrate the conquered elite into his empire. Roxana was not taken as a concubine or hostage, but as a queen, his equal by marriage, symbolic of the unity he sought between Greeks and Asians.

It was the first major step in his policy of fusion, which would later include the mass wedding at Susa and the training of Persian youths in Greek military fashion.

Through Roxana, Alexander made himself not only a conqueror of lands but a father to a new world.

City Building and Cultural Integration

As he subdued Central Asia, Alexander left behind more than destruction. He built cities, not just military outposts, and planned urban centers designed to spread Hellenic language, culture, and administration.

Among these were:

- Alexandria Eschate ('Alexandria the Furthest') in Sogdiana, near the Jaxartes River, his northeasternmost foundation.
- Several unnamed settlements in Bactria and across the Oxus, often settled with Macedonian veterans and local populations.

These cities served multiple purposes:

- Strategic control points to secure conquered regions.
- Cultural melting pots, where Greeks intermarried with locals.
- Trade hubs, facilitating economic ties from Greece to India.

In the barrenness of Central Asia, Alexander planted seeds of a new civilization. These cities would endure long after his death, preserving his legacy in places his successors would never fully control.

Suppression and Brutality

Still, it must be said: Alexander's campaign in Central Asia was among the most brutal of his career.

When Spitamenes threatened the region near Samarkand, Alexander dispatched forces under his general Coenus to pursue him. In 328 BC, Coenus defeated and killed Spitamenes, who had been betrayed by his own allies. In response, Alexander executed thousands of prisoners.

The war had dragged on for over two years. Alexander's tolerance diminished, his responses more ruthless. Rebellions were crushed with public executions. Cities were burned. Resistance was no longer treated as honorable but as treasonous.

He even executed Cleitus the Black, one of his oldest companions, in a drunken rage, an act that haunted him. The man who had saved his life at Granicus was struck down by the king he had followed across the known world.

The campaign in the east had changed Alexander. The boy who dreamed of Achilles was becoming something different, part general, part emperor, part myth.

Toward India: The End of the Central Asian Campaign

By the winter of 327 BC, Alexander had secured Bactria and Sogdiana, established cities, installed satraps, married into the local nobility, and eradicated large-scale resistance.

But he was not done.

He now turned his attention to the lands beyond the Hindu Kush, to the fabled riches of India, known to the Greeks only in legend. There, beyond the reach of Persia, lay a new challenge, a new enemy, and a new horizon.

Before leaving, Alexander ensured the region would be governed. He left trusted commanders in charge of Bactria, including Artabazus, and placed Roxana's father Oxyartes as satrap of the eastern provinces, an act of political consolidation through kinship.

The long Central Asian campaign, difficult and often thankless, had not brought him the glory of Gaugamela or the symbolism of Egypt, but it had been essential. Without it, the empire would have remained fragmented and vulnerable. With it, Alexander had built a corridor from the Aegean to the Jaxartes, a single chain of command, culture, and identity.

The campaign across Bactria and Sogdiana tested Alexander's resilience like no other. Here, he faced not empires with kings and capitals, but guerrilla resistance, tribal loyalties, and punishing terrain. It was a campaign not of swift victories but of relentless attrition, discipline, and adaptation.

By the time Alexander emerged from the highlands of Central Asia and crossed into India, he was no longer merely the son of Philip. He was Shahanshah, Pharaoh, Strategos, and king of the known world.

He had crossed into the heart of resistance and emerged with a dream intact: to create not just an empire of territory, but an empire of peoples, fused by conquest, sealed by marriage, and remembered forever.

CHAPTER 8. THE INDIAN CAMPAIGN

To the Edge of the World

By the spring of 327 BC, Alexander had conquered an empire that stretched from Macedon to the edges of Central Asia. The ancient power of Persia had fallen, the heartlands of Mesopotamia and Egypt lay under his control, and his name was spoken from the Aegean to the Oxus. But for Alexander, this was not the end. His mind burned with the same fire that had driven him from Pella as a boy, the need to see what lay beyond the next horizon, to push past the known and conquer the limits of the world.

And so he turned his army eastward, toward a mysterious and powerful land the Greeks knew only from legend, India.

What followed was one of the most extraordinary episodes in ancient military history: a perilous crossing of the Hindu Kush, a clash with a mighty Indian king, and, for the first time, resistance from within his own ranks. It was a campaign of daring, bloodshed, and revelation, and it brought Alexander closer to both glory and his human limits than ever before.

Crossing the Hindu Kush

To reach India, Alexander would have to traverse one of the harshest and most unforgiving terrains on Earth, the Hindu Kush Mountains.

Towering and treacherous, the Hindu Kush loomed like a natural fortress between Central Asia and the Indian subcontinent. Snowbound passes, thin air, freezing winds, and steep, rocky paths turned the journey into a trial of survival. Many of Alexander's men, already weary from years of campaigning, suffered frostbite, altitude sickness, and starvation.

Still, the army pushed forward, motivated by Alexander's unshakable will. His scouts guided them through narrow valleys and high passes. Horses and pack animals fell. Supplies dwindled. Yet Alexander pressed on, often marching alongside his soldiers on foot, enduring the same hardships, inspiring loyalty even as he tested their endurance.

When the army finally descended into the lush and fertile valleys of northern India, they entered a land unlike any they had seen: thick forests, towering rivers, elephant herds, and a rich, layered civilization that traced its roots back to the Indus Valley Civilization.

But what greeted them was not submission. It was resistance, and a king of formidable will.

The Battle of the Hydaspes (326 BC)

The Indian King

In the Punjab region, near the Hydaspes River (modern Jhelum, Pakistan), ruled King Porus, a powerful monarch of the Paurava kingdom. He was no petty prince. Towering in stature and commanding a seasoned army, Porus had sworn to resist Alexander's advance.

His force included war elephants, a terrifying new challenge for the Macedonian phalanx, as well as thousands of infantry and cavalry trained in Indian warfare. To Alexander, Porus was not merely another satrap, but a worthy and dangerous foe.

Indian war elephant against Alexander's troops by Johannes van den Avele, 1685

The Terrain and Strategy

The battle took place during the monsoon season, and the Hydaspes River was swollen and violent. Porus positioned his forces on the far side, assuming that Alexander would not risk a crossing during the storm.

But Alexander, as always, saw opportunity where others saw danger.

He led a detached force upstream under cover of night, using feints and diversions to distract Porus. At a shallow bend in the river, amid thunder and rain, Alexander crossed with a select force of cavalry and light infantry. They slipped across undetected.

Once across, he swiftly attacked Porus's left flank.

Caught by surprise, Porus sent reinforcements to meet the threat, but Alexander's elite Companion Cavalry smashed into the Indian lines with precision. As the battle raged, the main body of the Macedonian army, led by Craterus, crossed the river and struck from the front.

Porus's elephants crashed into the phalanx, creating chaos and carnage. Macedonian soldiers were trampled or thrown, horses panicked, and lines buckled. But Alexander's men adapted, targeting the mahouts, hamstringing the elephants, and using javelins to drive them back. In time, the great beasts turned wild and rampaged through Porus's own lines.

Despite being wounded and seeing his army collapse, Porus refused to flee. He fought until he was captured.

The Aftermath

Alexander, admiring Porus's valor, asked how he wished to be treated.

Porus is said to have replied, simply: 'As a king.'

Alexander was so impressed by his courage and dignity that he not only spared him but reinstated him as ruler, granting him even more territory than before. It was a move both pragmatic and noble. Porus became a loyal satrap and key ally in governing the Indian territories.

The Battle of the Hydaspes was one of Alexander's most difficult and costly victories. The Macedonians had never faced such terrain, elephants, or tactics. But it was also one of his most brilliant military achievements.

Still, this victory would mark a turning point, not in Alexander's conquests, but in the resolve of his army.

The Mutiny at the Hyphasis River

After the Hydaspes, Alexander pressed eastward toward the Hyphasis River (modern Beas), aiming to march to the Ganges, which he believed marked the edge of the world.

But here, his army finally refused to go further.

They had marched over 11,000 miles, fought in dozens of battles, crossed searing deserts and freezing mountains. Now, confronted with the knowledge of even larger kingdoms ahead, those of the Nanda dynasty in Magadha with vast armies and thousands of war elephants, his soldiers' resolve collapsed.

They gathered, weary and homesick, and confronted their king. Even the most loyal veterans, men who had followed him for a decade, refused to march.

Alexander, in fury and disbelief, withdrew to his tent for three days, refusing to eat or speak. He expected their resolve to break. But it didn't. The will of the army held firm.

At last, Alexander emerged and accepted reality. He performed sacrifices to the gods, symbolically marking the Hyphasis as the edge of his world, and built altars that stood for generations.

Then he ordered the army to turn west.

It was the first time Alexander's ambition had been outmatched by human limitation.

The Road Through the Gedrosian Desert

A Ruthless Decision

Alexander's decision to cross the Gedrosian Desert, a sun-scorched wasteland in present-day southeastern Iran and southern Pakistan, remains one of the most puzzling and criticized choices of his career.

Rather than taking the safer northern route through the Iranian plateau, Alexander led tens of thousands of men, women, and animals through the most desolate and dangerous route possible. Why?

Historians have long debated his motives:

- Was it to punish his army for mutinying at the Hyphasis?
- To match or surpass the failed desert march of Cyrus the Great?
- To explore a new coastal trade route alongside his fleet, commanded by Nearchus?

The truth may lie in a combination of all three. Alexander, driven by pride, curiosity, and strategy, sought to do the impossible, and paid dearly for it.

Hell on Earth

The Gedrosian Desert offered no forgiveness.

- Severe heat blistered the skin and scorched the ground.
- Wells were scarce, and when found, often brackish or dry.
- Supplies ran out, and men survived on crushed dates, cactus pulp, and rainwater caught in garments.
- Sandstorms buried men alive and disoriented columns.
- Thousands died, of thirst, disease, exhaustion, or madness.

Alexander is said to have shared the same water ration as his soldiers, even refusing a helmet full of water offered to him unless his men could also drink. Though his leadership inspired devotion, even he could not prevent disaster.

Entire pack animals perished. Camp followers collapsed on the dunes. Skeletons bleached in the sun. Some estimates claim that up to three-quarters of his troops and attendants died in the desert crossing.

When Alexander finally emerged from the wilderness into Carmania, the survivors wept, not for joy, but for those they had lost.

Wider Impact of the Indian Campaign

Despite the hardships, Alexander's Indian campaign left a lasting legacy.

- Greek settlements were established in the region, such as Alexandria Bucephala, named after Alexander's beloved horse Bucephalus, who died after the Battle of the Hydaspes.
- The exchange of cultures, ideas, and trade between India and the West was accelerated by his presence.
- The campaign left such an impression that Greek rule persisted in parts of India for over two centuries through the Indo-Greek kingdoms.
- Indian sources, though sparse, refer to Alexander as 'Yavana', meaning Greek, and preserve fragments of his legacy, especially through Buddhist and Jain chronicles.

His Indian adventure was brief, less than two years, but its influence rippled across centuries, opening new connections between east and west.

Alexander came to India searching for glory, discovery, and the limits of the earth. He found all three.

He faced his fiercest battle, won over a formidable rival, and witnessed his army's humanity. At the Hyphasis, he learned that even gods cannot command endlessly.

And yet, what he achieved in India was extraordinary. He extended his empire farther than any before him, forged bonds with Indian rulers, and planted the seeds of Hellenistic culture thousands of miles from Greece.

But India also marked a shift, from expansion to introspection. As he turned west, the man who had raced toward the horizon now began to look backward, toward legacy, consolidation, and, perhaps unknowingly, toward death.

For Alexander, the conquest of India was not just a geographical journey, it was the end of one world and the beginning of another.

PART IV: THE FINAL CHAPTER

CHAPTER 9. RETURN THROUGH HARDSHIP

Sand, Strategy, and the Seeds of Empire

The Euphrates flowed broad and serene, a lifeline through the dusty heat of Mesopotamia. When Alexander returned to Babylon in 324 BC, he was no longer just a conqueror. He was a man who had walked through fire, through rivers and jungles, over mountain passes, and across deserts that swallowed whole armies. Behind him lay the most perilous campaign of his life, a march not through enemy territory, but through the vast emptiness of the Gedrosian Desert, where ambition nearly met its end.

Alexander's return west from India was not one of triumphant retreat but of ordeal and transformation. It was during this final phase that he faced resistance from his own men, wrestled with the challenge of governing a multi-ethnic empire, and made bold, controversial efforts to merge the Greek and Persian worlds into one.

The man who emerged from this crucible was no longer simply the King of Macedon. He was the architect of something new, an empire without precedent, forged by hardship, sustained by vision, and haunted by mortality.

The Carmanian Interlude

In Carmania (modern southeastern Iran), Alexander held a celebration of survival after the horrors of the Gedrosian Desert, described by some sources as a strange and symbolic procession:

- Soldiers dressed in leaves and vines, pulling wagons of wine.
- Musicians played flutes and lyres.
- Alexander and his officers rode in gilded chariots, drunk and sunburnt, still reeling from the ordeal.

It was a moment of release after months of death and despair, a grim victory parade for surviving nature itself.

But it also marked a shift. From here, Alexander's campaign took on a new purpose: to solidify the empire, bind together East and West, and transform from a conquering warlord into a universal monarch.

Integration of Persian Troops

The 'New Alexander'

From the moment he entered the Persian court at Persepolis, Alexander had begun adopting Achaemenid customs: Persian dress, court rituals, even the practice of proskynesis, bowing or kneeling before the king. While these gestures were natural to his new eastern subjects, they infuriated many of his Macedonian companions.

But Alexander had outgrown Macedon. He was no longer a king of one people. He ruled over an empire of Greeks, Persians, Babylonians, Egyptians, Sogdians, and now Indians. To hold it together, he needed more than military might, he needed cultural legitimacy.

The Arrival of the Epigoni

One of his boldest moves came during the return from India. In preparation for future campaigns (perhaps into Arabia), Alexander had ordered the training of a new corps of Persian youths in the Macedonian military style. These young men, the Epigoni ('Successors'), were taught Greek, drilled in the phalanx, and adopted Macedonian weaponry.

In 324 BC, 30,000 of them marched to join the army in Susa.

Their arrival shocked the veterans. Many Macedonians, already jealous of Alexander's eastern policies, now feared they were being replaced. The symbolism was stark: the conqueror's army now included those they had conquered.

This culminated in the 'mutiny at Opis.' Macedonian soldiers, furious at being dismissed or sidelined in favor of Persians, openly revolted.

The Opis Mutiny

Alexander's response was chilling. He dismissed the entire Macedonian army, declaring he no longer needed them, and would instead rely on the loyal Persians. The veterans, stunned and remorseful, begged for forgiveness.

Alexander eventually relented, weeping in front of his men and reuniting them under his command. He then held a massive banquet of unity with Macedonian and Persian officers dining side by side, a symbolic gesture toward the blended empire he envisioned.

But the incident revealed the growing tension between old loyalties and new ambitions. Alexander was reshaping the very identity of his army, and, by extension, his empire.

Administrative Reforms and Fusion

Dual Governance

To govern his vast and diverse territories, Alexander implemented a system of dual administration:

- In many provinces, he appointed both a Macedonian commander and a local satrap.

- This ensured both military control and cultural continuity.

- Local laws and customs were often preserved, as long as taxes were paid and loyalty to Alexander maintained.

This strategy, modeled in part on Persian governance, allowed for relative stability across thousands of miles. It also allowed Alexander to claim legitimacy not as a foreign tyrant, but as the rightful heir of Darius.

The Susa Weddings

One of Alexander's most symbolic acts of fusion took place in 324 BC, in the Persian capital of Susa. There, he held a mass wedding ceremony:

- Over 80 Macedonian officers married Persian noblewomen in a grand display of unity.

- Alexander himself took two more wives: Stateira, the daughter of Darius III, and Parysatis, the daughter of Artaxerxes III, thus tying himself directly to the Achaemenid royal line.

- Roxana, his Bactrian wife, remained his first queen.

These weddings were meant to cement the bonds between conqueror and conquered, between the Greek and Persian elites. Alexander promised generous dowries and gifts. The goal was clear: to build an aristocracy of blended blood that could carry forward his vision.

Yet many Macedonians resented these unions, seeing them as betrayals of Hellenic identity.

After Alexander's death, most of the marriages were repudiated.

A New Imperial Capital: Babylon

Alexander's return to Babylon in late 324 BC marked a turning point. He had traveled to the edge of the known world and returned, alive but changed.

Alexander the Great in Babylon

From this ancient city, rich in wealth, history, and cosmopolitanism, he planned to make the administrative heart of his empire. Babylon's strategic location at the crossroads of trade and its symbolic importance made it ideal.

- He began organizing tax systems and satrapal boundaries.

- Commissioned canals and infrastructure to link his empire's breadbaskets.

- Appointed Persian and Greek officials in tandem, hoping to create a hybrid bureaucracy.

- Continued to send Greek settlers east and bring eastern soldiers west.

There were even plans for a new campaign, perhaps against Arabia or Carthage. The Mediterranean and Indian Ocean might yet be joined under one banner.

But Alexander's body, stretched by battle, march, and vision, had limits.

And time was running out.

The Legacy of Fusion

Alexander's efforts to integrate the peoples of his empire went far beyond marriage and military.

- He founded over twenty cities, many of which became thriving centers of Greek and local culture.

- He encouraged multilingual education, commerce, and the translation of texts.

- Greek art, coinage, architecture, and drama spread across Asia, while Eastern dress, titles, and court customs found their way back to the Mediterranean.

What he envisioned was not a Macedonian empire, but a cosmopolitan civilization, bound not by race or language, but by allegiance to one sovereign vision.

He failed to fully realize it in his lifetime, but his dream would echo in the Hellenistic kingdoms that followed, in the fusion of ideas that gave rise to Greco-Buddhist art, and in the cities like Alexandria, Antioch, and Ai-Khanoum, where cultures met and transformed.

Fire and Vision

The return through hardship was not merely physical. Alexander's desert crossing, military reforms, and cultural fusion marked a turning point in his reign, from conqueror to emperor, from battlefield genius to ambitious world-builder.

But the unity he sought came at a price. His men grew restless. His companions muttered about his foreign ways. His empire, though vast, remained fragile, held together by his charisma, will, and genius.

In Babylon, as he worked feverishly to complete his plans, fate intervened. Fever struck. The man who had survived every battle, every rebellion, and even the deserts of Gedrosia, now lay dying.

But that final chapter, his death and legacy, would not silence his story. For Alexander had already ensured that the world he left behind would never be the same again.

CHAPTER 10. DEATH IN BABYLON

The Unfinished Empire

The heart of Alexander the Great's empire beat in Babylon, and Alexander's vision of a united world seemed closer than ever.

But it was also in Babylon, surrounded by the luxury of Persian palaces and the echoes of his great victories, that Alexander's life abruptly came to an end. The suddenness of his death, at the age of just 32, shocked the world and left his generals, his soldiers, and his empire in a state of disarray.

Plans for Arabia and Beyond

As Alexander lingered in Babylon during the spring and early summer of 323 BC, he was not idle. Far from it, he was planning his next conquest, which he saw as both a natural extension of his vision and an opportunity to complete the legacy he had begun in India.

The next target on his list was Arabia.

The Importance of Arabia

Arabia had long been a land of mystery and myth for the Greeks and Persians alike. The deserts were harsh and largely unexplored by the West, but Alexander had heard of the riches and power that lay within. He believed that Arabia, with its strategic location and access to the Red Sea and the Indian Ocean, was the next logical conquest after India. But more than that, it was symbolic. He envisioned it as the final piece of his universal empire, uniting both East and West under a single banner.

Moreover, Alexander had already set his sights on expanding global trade routes through Arabia, establishing new networks that would link his empire from the Mediterranean to the Indian subcontinent. An Arabian campaign would consolidate his rule and open access to even more riches, particularly in the form of trade in spices, incense, and precious stones.

The Strategic Imperative

By 323 BC, Alexander had appointed Nearchus to oversee naval expeditions and sent other generals to ensure the flow of resources and manpower from Greece, Persia, and India. The campaign to Arabia would be an attempt to control key trade routes and further assert Greek dominance in an increasingly diverse world.

Beyond that, Alexander's restless nature was evident: he wanted to push the boundaries even further. He had been thwarted by the mutiny at the Hyphasis River in India, but in his mind, the Arabian desert was a much more controllable landscape. Arabian tribes, while fiercely independent, were no match for the might of Alexander's army. His vision of global unification demanded that he leave no corner of the earth unconquered.

Yet, these plans would remain unfinished, as fate would intervene in the most unexpected of ways.

Sudden Illness and Death in 323 BC

The events surrounding Alexander's death remain a source of intrigue and speculation. On the night of June 10, 323 BC, Alexander was struck down by a sudden illness. The details of his illness are murky and have been the subject of historical debate for millennia. According to ancient sources, Alexander fell ill after a banquet in the palace of Nebuchadnezzar II in Babylon, where he had been celebrating a series of recent victories.

At first, the symptoms seemed minor. Alexander complained of a fever, which worsened over the next few days. The fever became high, and he became physically weak. For a man who had conquered the world, the sickness came with astonishing swiftness and intensity. He was bedridden for several days, unable to speak or move, though some sources mention that he remained conscious during the initial stages of the illness.

The final days of Alexander's life were marked by confusion, fear, and uncertainty. Some of his close companions and generals were desperately trying to find a remedy, consulting doctors, diviners, and sorcerers. The court in Babylon was thrown into turmoil. The question was not just how to save Alexander's life, but what would become of the empire without him.

On June 13, after twelve days of suffering, Alexander died in the royal palace, his body left in a state of cold sweat and trembling. He was just 32 years old.

Theories About His Death

Over the centuries, numerous theories have emerged to explain the untimely death of Alexander the Great. These theories range from natural causes to poisoning, and each one reflects the complex political and social landscape surrounding Alexander's death.

Natural Causes

The most commonly accepted explanation by modern historians is that Alexander died of a fever caused by a natural illness. Some scholars suggest that he may have succumbed to malaria or typhoid fever, both of which were common in the region at the time. The symptoms of these diseases match the fever and the weakness that Alexander exhibited in his final days.

Malaria, in particular, was prevalent in the swampy regions near Babylon, and the ancient sources describe Alexander's fever as having episodic surges, which is characteristic of malaria. Typhoid fever, caused by contaminated water, was also widespread in ancient Babylon. These diseases, compounded by Alexander's exhaustion from years of military campaigns, could have easily led to his rapid demise.

Poisoning

Another theory that has persisted for centuries is that Alexander was poisoned. This theory often comes from the dramatic and suspicious circumstances surrounding Alexander's death, his sudden illness, the fact that no doctor could save him, and the political implications of his death. The idea of poisoning is particularly appealing given the power struggles that followed his death.

Several ancient authors, including Plutarch and Justin, mention the possibility of foul play, with some alleging that Antipater, a high-ranking officer and father of the influential general Cassander, had a motive to eliminate Alexander. Antipater had his own ambitions, and the idea of a poisoned drink, perhaps slipped into Alexander's wine during the banquet, is one of the most enduring theories. However, it is important to note that the timeline of poisoning would not perfectly align with Alexander's symptoms, and the idea of poisoning remains speculative.

Divine Retribution

Some ancient writers suggested that Alexander's death was a form of divine retribution. His remarkable success and divine pretensions, such as his claim to be the son of Zeus-Ammon and his adoption of Persian royal customs, may have angered the gods, who then punished him for his perceived hubris. This view was particularly common among those who opposed his efforts to blend Greek and Persian cultures.

For example, Plutarch references a mysterious prophecy which stated that Alexander would die in the 'same year as his father.' In some circles, this became interpreted as a sign of divine displeasure for the breaking of natural order.

Exhaustion and Stress

There is also the possibility that Alexander's death was simply the result of his relentless pursuit of conquest. His physically and mentally taxing campaigns, combined with his personal stress, might have pushed his body beyond its limits. After years of nearly continuous warfare, endless marching, and strategic manipulation, the young king may have finally succumbed to the toll of his lifestyle.

Alexander's constant drive for more, his insatiable ambition, and the psychological weight of being the self-proclaimed 'King of the World', could have triggered a collapse in his health. The demands of ruling an empire that spanned three continents, with countless cultures and peoples, may have left him vulnerable to an illness that would have otherwise been manageable.

After Alexander's Death

Alexander's triggered not only a power struggle for his vast empire but also a dramatic and mysterious saga around his body, tomb, and final resting place, a tale laced with political intrigue, ambition, and legend.

Death and Embalming: The Legend Begins

Alexander's body did not receive a swift burial. According to ancient sources, including Diodorus Siculus and Quintus Curtius Rufus, his corpse was embalmed, possibly in honey or some other preservative, as was common in Mesopotamian and Egyptian practices. The delay in burial was partly due to political uncertainty and partly because the body itself was seen as a powerful symbol of sovereignty.

In the ancient world, possession of a king's body often meant political legitimacy. As no clear successor had been appointed, Alexander's generals and satraps quickly realized that controlling his remains could bolster their claims to authority.

The Funeral Cortege and Its Seizure

Alexander's body was reportedly placed in a magnificent golden sarcophagus and an elaborate funeral cart, described as a grand, wheeled structure adorned with columns, gold, and divine imagery, befitting a god-king.

Funeral Cart of Alexander the Great

Initially, the funeral procession was supposed to transport his remains back to Macedon, to be laid to rest in the royal tombs of his ancestors at Aegae (modern Vergina in northern Greece). However, Ptolemy, one of Alexander's most capable generals and future ruler of Egypt, had other plans.

Around 321 BCE, Ptolemy intercepted the funeral cortege in Syria (likely near Damascus). He diverted it to Egypt, possibly with the tacit support of Perdiccas, the regent of the empire at the time. This bold move had enormous political significance: Ptolemy was staking a claim to Alexander's legacy by possessing the king's remains.

Burial in Memphis and Move to Alexandria

Initially, Ptolemy buried Alexander in Memphis, the old capital of Egypt. Memphis held symbolic importance, linking Alexander with the pharaonic traditions and divine legitimacy. Later, either Ptolemy I or his son Ptolemy II transferred Alexander's remains to Alexandria, the city Alexander had founded, and which had since become the capital of Ptolemaic Egypt.

There, a grand mausoleum known as the Soma or Sema was constructed to house Alexander's body. It was located in the heart of Alexandria, likely near the royal palace district. The tomb became a pilgrimage site, visited by notable figures including:

- Julius Caesar, who reportedly viewed the body during his time in Egypt.

- Augustus, who is said to have placed a golden crown on Alexander's mummified head.

- Caligula, who allegedly stole Alexander's breastplate for himself.

Disappearance and Mystery of the Tomb

By the 4th or 5th century AD, Alexander's tomb vanished from historical records. Several theories attempt to explain this mystery:

- It may have been destroyed during riots, earthquakes, or the rise of Christianity and the suppression of pagan sites.

- It could have been buried beneath the modern city of Alexandria, which has experienced substantial urban development over centuries.

- Some believe it lies under a mosque or another building in modern Alexandria.

Despite numerous archaeological efforts, Alexander's tomb has never been definitively found.

Symbolic and Political Significance

Ptolemy's seizure of Alexander's body was more than opportunistic theft, it was a calculated political act:

- It linked Ptolemy to Alexander's divine status, boosting his claim to rule Egypt.

- It turned Alexandria into a spiritual and imperial center, reinforcing the legitimacy of the new dynasty.

- It symbolized the shift in power from Macedon to the Hellenistic East.

The tomb itself became a centerpiece of dynastic propaganda, enshrining Alexander not only as a conquering hero but as a quasi-divine founder.

Final Mystery

Where is Alexander's tomb today? Despite numerous claims and expeditions, ranging from beneath Alexandria's Latin Cemetery to Siwa Oasis, the location remains unknown. The mystery of his final resting place adds another layer of immortality to his legend, as even in death, Alexander eludes final discovery.

Reactions of His Generals and Empire

The death of Alexander in 323 BC created an immediate crisis. He had left no clear heir, and the question of who would rule the vast empire he had created became an urgent and bitterly contested issue. Several factors complicated the situation further:

The Absence of an Heir

At the time of his death, Alexander's only legitimate heir was his infant son, Alexander IV, who was born to his wife Roxana shortly after his death. However, the child was far too young to govern, and the generals quickly recognized that power would need to be consolidated in the hands of one or more regents.

The Diadochi: The Struggle for Power

Alexander's death set off a power struggle among his most trusted generals, known as the Diadochi ('Successors'). Among them were figures such as Ptolemy, who seized control of Egypt; Seleucus, who eventually founded the Seleucid Empire in the East; Antigonus, who sought to control Asia Minor and much of the eastern territories; and Cassander, who controlled Macedon.

This period of infighting, known as the Wars of the Diadochi, would last for decades and eventually fragment Alexander's empire into several Hellenistic kingdoms. His dream of a unified empire collapsed as his generals carved out their own domains and established their own dynasties.

The Legacy of a King

Alexander the Great's death was a monumental event, marking not just the end of a remarkable life but also the end of an era. His legacy, however, would live on. His military genius, vision of unity, and the cultural fusion he initiated would leave a lasting imprint on the world. The Hellenistic period that followed his death would see Greek culture spread across much of Asia and North Africa, laying the foundation for the Roman Empire and influencing civilizations for centuries.

Though his empire fragmented quickly after his death, the idea of Alexander would endure, his ambition and drive to unite the known world, even if he could not complete it in his lifetime.

PART V: THE WORLD AFTER ALEXANDER

CHAPTER 11. THE WARS OF THE SUCCESSORS

The Fragmentation of the Empire

Upon Alexander's death, his empire was left without a clear heir. His only legitimate heir was his infant son, Alexander IV, born to Roxana, his Bactrian wife. However, the child was only a few months old and utterly incapable of ruling. In the immediate aftermath of Alexander's death, his generals recognized that power would need to be consolidated among themselves, as Alexander had not left a clear dynastic succession.

The empire was vast and diverse, encompassing Greek, Persian, Egyptian, and Indian territories. Its political and administrative structure was fragile, relying on the personality and genius of Alexander himself. Without him, the different parts of the empire began to break away, as each general sought to control regions that were strategically and culturally important to them.

The Regency of Perdiccas

In the early months after Alexander's death, the generals agreed to make Perdiccas, a high-ranking officer in Alexander's army, the regent for the young Alexander IV. He was tasked with overseeing the empire until the child was old enough to rule. Perdiccas also took control of the royal treasury and assumed the authority to manage the empire's military affairs.

However, Perdiccas's rule was disputed from the beginning. Many of Alexander's generals saw him as an outsider, and his authority was questioned. Ptolemy, the commander of Alexander's Egyptian forces, quickly became a rival to Perdiccas. Seleucus, who commanded the forces in Mesopotamia, also eyed his own share of the empire. Meanwhile, Antipater, the governor of Macedon, and Antigonus, a seasoned general, were also deeply invested in securing power for themselves.

The Division of the Empire

The Diadochi were a group of men who had been close companions of Alexander. Their loyalty to him was unquestioned during his lifetime, but once he was gone, their personal ambition soon took precedence. These men had grown powerful through their military exploits and their ability to command large armies.

By 321 BC, the empire had been divided into several territories, each controlled by one of Alexander's generals. These divisions were informal at first, as the generals fought for dominance.

The division of the empire sparked immediate conflict. The generals saw each other as both allies and rivals, and old alliances quickly broke down. The empire that Alexander had built began to disintegrate as the Diadochi engaged in a series of wars, the Wars of the Successors, for control of different territories.

The kingdoms that were established as a result, though politically fragmented, shared a common Greek heritage and contributed to the spread of Hellenistic culture, including art, philosophy, science, and architecture. The Hellenistic period was defined by cultural exchange and intellectual flourishing, as Greek ideas spread across Egypt, Persia, and India.

The following figures would emerge as the dominant players in the struggle for control of Alexander's empire.

Ptolemy I Soter (Egypt)

Ptolemy, one of Alexander's most trusted generals, was given control of Egypt. He quickly realized the strategic value of Egypt and its rich resources. Seizing upon the lack of strong central authority, Ptolemy proclaimed himself king of Egypt in 305 BC, founding the Ptolemaic dynasty that would last for nearly 300 years. He built a powerful and prosperous kingdom centered around Alexandria, which became a major center of Greek culture, trade, and learning.

Ptolemy also took control of Cyprus and Palestine, becoming a formidable force in the eastern Mediterranean. He was adept at diplomacy and military strategy, and under his rule, Egypt became a stronghold of Greek culture and influence.

Seleucus I Nicator (Mesopotamia and Persia)

Seleucus established control over Babylon, Persia, and much of Asia. In 312 BC, Seleucus faced a major challenge from Antigonus, who sought to control the entire eastern part of the empire. Seleucus's campaign against Antigonus culminated in the Battle of Ipsus in 301 BC, where Antigonus was defeated and killed. This victory allowed Seleucus to expand his territories, and he eventually founded the Seleucid Empire, which stretched from Syria to India.

The Seleucid Empire became a powerful Hellenistic kingdom, although it faced constant pressure from both internal revolts and external threats from the Parthians. Nonetheless, Seleucus's legacy endured through his descendants, who ruled much of the Near East for centuries.

Antigonus I Monophthalmus (Asia Minor and Syria)

Antigonus, known as 'the One-Eyed', was one of Alexander's most formidable commanders. He sought to reunite the empire and proclaimed himself King of Asia. Antigonus made significant gains, particularly in Asia Minor and Syria, but his ambitions led him into conflict with the other Diadochi.

In 301 BC, Antigonus was defeated by the combined forces of Seleucus and Lysimachus at the Battle of Ipsus. Antigonus was killed in the battle, and his territories were divided among the victorious generals. Although Antigonus's dynasty was short-lived, his name endured as a symbol of the ambition and power that defined the Wars of the Successors.

Cassander (Macedon and Greece)

Cassander, who had been entrusted with ruling Macedon and Greece, was a key figure in the early Wars of the Successors. He had been a close companion of Alexander, but his ambitions led him to bitter conflict with the other Diadochi. Cassander eventually took control of Macedon in 317 BC, after a protracted war against Antipater's son, Olympias (Alexander's mother).

Cassander's rule marked the beginning of the Antipatrid dynasty in Macedon. Although he was unable to secure control over all of Greece, he was able to retain power in Macedon and secure the Ptolemaic and Seleucid alliances, ensuring that his position as king remained unchallenged.

The Deaths of Roxana and Alexander IV

As the Wars of the Successors raged on, the fates of Roxana and Alexander IV, Alexander's widow and son, took tragic turns. Both were regarded as symbols of Alexander's legacy, but they had little political power.

Roxana's Fate

Roxana was left in a precarious position after his death. With Alexander IV being an infant, Roxana was initially placed under the protection of Perdiccas, the regent. However, after Perdiccas's death in 321 BC, the situation quickly deteriorated. In 316 BC, Cassander, seeking to secure his own position, ordered the execution of Roxana. She was murdered in a plot orchestrated by Cassander, along with her son, Alexander IV.

The Fate of Alexander IV

Alexander IV, who had been born after his father's death, was the last living heir to Alexander's empire. As a young child, he had no ability to govern, and his fate was sealed by the power struggles around him. After the murder of his mother, Cassander ensured that Alexander IV would never rule. In 310 BC, after a failed attempt to use the child as a political pawn, Alexander IV was executed, marking the official end of the Argead dynasty.

CHAPTER 12. THE HELLENISTIC AGE

A World Transformed

The death of Alexander the Great marked not the end of his empire, but the beginning of an era that would forever alter the course of history. Though his empire was fragmented by the Wars of the Successors, his vision of a unified world, where East and West would merge, lived on. The Hellenistic Age, spanning from Alexander's death to the rise of the Roman Empire, is defined by the spread of Greek culture across three continents and the creation of a new world order in which Greek ideas would merge with local traditions and give rise to a new era of philosophy, science, and art.

Though his empire splintered into Hellenistic kingdoms, Alexander's legacy was reflected in the blending of cultures that characterized this age. The Greek language, once confined to the Mediterranean, became the lingua franca of the East, from the Aegean to the Indus River. Greek art, drama, and philosophy spread far and wide, shaping societies from Egypt to India. At the same time, the interaction of Greek and Eastern traditions gave rise to a new syncretic culture that blended the old with the new.

Spread of Greek Language and Ideas

One of the most enduring legacies of Alexander's conquests was the spread of the Greek language. As Alexander's armies marched eastward, they brought Greek culture and institutions with them. Under Alexander's rule, Greek became the language of administration, trade, and intellectual exchange across the vast reaches of his empire. Even after his death, the spread of Greek language and thought continued to flourish under the Hellenistic monarchs who inherited his territories.

Greek as the Lingua Franca

Greek became the dominant language of communication from Egypt to the Indian subcontinent, as it was used in official documents, trade, and education. In cities like Alexandria and Antioch, Greek was the common tongue spoken by the elite and intellectual classes. This linguistic unification allowed ideas to circulate freely, from the Mediterranean to the farthest reaches of Central Asia and beyond.

The Hellenization of the East was not only linguistic but also cultural. The cities Alexander founded, including Alexandria in Egypt and Seleucia in Mesopotamia, became melting pots where Greek settlers, Persian subjects, Egyptians, Jews, and Indians lived together, creating a cosmopolitan culture. Greek ideas in art, architecture, and science mingled with the local traditions, creating a distinctive Hellenistic style that would influence civilizations for centuries.

The Greek language remained the medium for intellectual and artistic expression in the Eastern Mediterranean. In cities such as Alexandria, Antioch, and Pergamon, Greek philosophers, scientists, and artists continued to flourish, contributing to an era of cultural achievement that would shape the future of Western civilization.

Greek Philosophy Spreads East

Greek philosophy, which had once been confined to the intellectual circles of Athens and the Greek-speaking world, spread throughout the Hellenistic kingdoms. The mystical and logical systems developed by Greek philosophers found fertile ground in the diverse, cosmopolitan cities of the East. The merging of Greek philosophical traditions with Persian and Egyptian thought produced new schools of philosophy, each of which would shape the intellectual landscape for centuries.

Philosophers like Aristotle and Plato continued to have an enduring influence on the Greek-speaking world, but it was during the Hellenistic period that new philosophical schools began to emerge, reflecting the complex nature of the new, multicultural world Alexander had created.

Alexandria and the Scientific Golden Age

Perhaps the greatest testament to Alexander's legacy in the Hellenistic world was the city of Alexandria in Egypt. Founded by Alexander, Alexandria quickly became the intellectual and cultural capital of the Hellenistic world. Under the rule of the Ptolemies, Alexandria became home to a vast library and museum, attracting scholars and thinkers from across the Greek-speaking world and beyond.

The Library of Alexandria

The Library of Alexandria, founded by Ptolemy I and later expanded by Ptolemy II, became the largest and most important library in the ancient world. It housed hundreds of thousands of scrolls, covering subjects ranging from mathematics to medicine, astronomy to literature. Scholars came from all corners of the known world to study in the library's halls, making Alexandria the center of intellectual activity during the Hellenistic period.

The library not only preserved Greek knowledge but also sought to gather the works of ancient civilizations, from Egyptian texts to Babylonian astronomy. Scholars such as Euclid, the father of geometry, and Archimedes, the brilliant mathematician and inventor, worked in Alexandria, making discoveries that would lay the foundation for future scientific progress.

Scientific Advancements

Under the Ptolemies, Alexandria became the epicenter of scientific discovery. The city attracted some of the greatest minds of the time, including Eratosthenes, who calculated the circumference of the Earth with remarkable accuracy, and Hipparchus, who created the first star catalog and made pioneering work in the field of astronomy.

The scientific advancements made in Alexandria were not confined to theory. Alexandrian scholars worked on practical inventions, such as Archimedes' screw, an apparatus for lifting water, and the compound pulley, which greatly impacted the development of engineering techniques in the ancient world. Alexandria's thriving intellectual scene would continue to influence both the Roman Empire and the Byzantine Empire, ensuring that its legacy lived on for centuries.

Cultural and Intellectual Exchange

As a city at the crossroads of East and West, Alexandria was not just a Greek city but a melting pot of various cultures, including Egyptian, Persian, and Jewish communities. This diversity fostered an environment in which ideas could flow freely, and intellectual exchange occurred between Greek and non-Greek scholars. Philosophers, scientists, mathematicians, and poets all found their place in Alexandria, leading to a golden age of scientific and cultural achievement.

One of the most notable intellectual exchanges in Alexandria was the interaction between Greek and Egyptian thought. Egyptian priests influenced Greek thinkers, while Greek ideas transformed the way Egyptians approached knowledge. This blending of ideas was not only confined to science but also affected the development of religion, art, and literature in the Hellenistic world.

Cultural Exchange Between East and West

The Hellenistic Age was one of profound cultural exchange. As Greek culture spread across the vast territories of Alexander's empire, it encountered and interacted with Eastern and Persian cultures, leading to a dynamic process of cultural amalgamation. The fusion of Greek and local traditions produced a new Hellenistic civilization that was markedly different from classical Greek culture.

Art and Architecture

The blending of Greek and Eastern cultures was most visible in the art and architecture of the Hellenistic world. Greek-inspired styles were combined with local elements to create a distinctive Hellenistic artistic tradition. The most famous example of this fusion is the creation of Hellenistic sculpture, which focused on realism, emotion, and movement, a stark contrast to the idealized forms of classical Greek art. Statues like the Laocoön and the Venus de Milo exemplify this new style, which sought to capture the human experience in a more lifelike manner.

Architecturally, Hellenistic cities like Alexandria, Antioch, and Pergamon incorporated Greek columns and temples but also adopted local building techniques and designs. The Alexandrian Lighthouse (Pharos) is one of the Seven Wonders of the Ancient World and showcases both Greek engineering and Egyptian influence in its design.

Religion and Syncretism

The Hellenistic period also saw the fusion of Greek gods and Eastern deities. In Egypt, the Greek gods were merged with Egyptian gods, leading to the creation of new syncretic deities like Serapis, who combined attributes of Osiris, Zeus, and Hades. In India, Greek deities were blended with local Hindu gods, resulting in the Greco-Buddhist art that flourished in the Gandhara region.

The spread of Greek culture did not erase local traditions but rather merged them with Greek influences, creating a rich tapestry of religious and cultural practices that continued to evolve throughout the Hellenistic period.

Rise of Stoicism, Epicureanism, and New Philosophies

The Hellenistic Age was not only an era of cultural exchange but also one of profound philosophical development. With the collapse of the Greek city-state system and the rise of new Hellenistic kingdoms, philosophers began to shift their focus from political theory to questions of ethics and individual fulfillment. Two of the most influential philosophical schools to emerge during this period were Stoicism and Epicureanism.

Stoicism

Founded by Zeno of Citium in Athens around 300 BC, Stoicism taught that virtue and happiness could be achieved by living in accordance with nature and accepting the inevitable flow of events. Stoics believed that human beings were part of a rational universe and that by controlling their emotions and desires, they could achieve peace of mind. Stoicism became widely influential in the Hellenistic world and later in the Roman Empire, particularly with figures such as Seneca, Epictetus, and the Emperor Marcus Aurelius.

Epicureanism

In contrast to Stoicism, Epicureanism, founded by Epicurus, emphasized the pursuit of pleasure and the absence of pain as the ultimate goal of life. Epicurus taught that simple pleasures, such as friendship and contemplation, were the key to happiness. Unlike the hedonistic excesses often associated with pleasure, Epicureanism promoted a life of moderation and intellectual fulfillment. The philosophy was appealing to many in the Hellenistic world, particularly in the cities of Alexandria and Athens.

PART IV: LEGACY AND LEGEND

CHAPTER 13. MILITARY GENIUS

The Strategic Brilliance of Alexander the Great

The legacy of Alexander the Great is inextricably tied to his unparalleled achievements as a military commander. In just over a decade of campaigning, he created one of the largest empires in history, stretching from Macedon to the Indus River. His strategic genius, tactical innovation, and remarkable leadership have made him a model for military commanders throughout history, including figures as diverse as Julius Caesar, Napoleon Bonaparte, and modern military leaders. Alexander's undefeated record and his ability to conquer vast, diverse territories at an astonishing pace remain defining elements of his legacy. In this chapter, we will delve into the tactics and strategies that made Alexander such a formidable force on the battlefield, examine his leadership style, and explore how his influence has endured through the centuries.

The Foundations of Alexander's Military Genius

Training and Early Experience

Before his historic campaigns, Alexander had been carefully groomed for leadership by his father, Philip II, who transformed Macedon into a formidable military power. From a young age, Alexander was exposed to military strategy and tactics, learning from his father's successes and failures. Under Philip's tutelage, Alexander received an elite education in both philosophy and warfare, studying under renowned thinkers like Aristotle, which helped him hone his understanding of strategy, politics, and human nature.

However, it was during the Battle of Chaeronea in 338 BC, when Alexander was just 18, that he first demonstrated his exceptional military instincts. Leading the Macedonian cavalry to a decisive victory against the Greek city-states, Alexander's actions marked the beginning of his reputation as a brilliant strategist and tactician. This victory not only cemented his place as a leader in Macedon but also laid the groundwork for his future campaigns against the Persian Empire.

Strategic Brilliance: The Art of War

Alexander's military strategy was rooted in his ability to adapt to the specific challenges of each battlefield. He was never rigid in his approach; rather, he combined his knowledge of different combat techniques and adjusted his tactics to exploit the weaknesses of his enemies. Some key elements of his strategic brilliance included mobility, deception, and the ability to maintain discipline under pressure.

The Use of Mobility

One of Alexander's key strategies was the use of speed and mobility. His armies were highly mobile, with cavalry playing a central role in his tactics. The Macedonian phalanx, a formation of infantry armed with sarissas (long spears), was complemented by swift cavalry units, particularly the Companion Cavalry, which Alexander himself led into battle. This combination allowed him to strike decisively, often before his enemies could react.

Alexander's armies were able to travel long distances quickly, which caught many of his enemies off guard. For example, in the Battle of Gaugamela (331 BC), Alexander moved his army with remarkable speed, allowing him to outflank and decimate the Persian forces despite their superior numbers. His ability to move his troops swiftly and strike with precision gave him a significant advantage over more traditional, slower-moving armies.

Deception and Psychological Warfare

Alexander was also a master of psychological warfare. He often employed deceptive tactics to mislead his enemies and create confusion. One of the most notable examples of this occurred during the siege of Tyre in 332 BC, when he built a causeway to the island city. The Tyrians believed that their island position made them safe from the siege, but Alexander's use of innovative engineering, combined with his ability to anticipate his enemies' reactions, forced the city to surrender after several months of intense fighting.

Alexander understood that morale played a crucial role in warfare. By leading his troops from the front and demonstrating his fearlessness, he inspired loyalty and courage among his soldiers. His personal involvement in battles, particularly his habit of charging into the thick of the fight, helped maintain a strong bond between him and his troops, further contributing to their effectiveness.

Adaptability and Flexibility

Another hallmark of Alexander's strategy was his ability to adapt to new challenges and change his approach as necessary. This adaptability was evident in his campaigns against the Persian Empire and later in India, where he faced vastly different terrain and enemies. In the Battle of Issus (333 BC), for example, Alexander used the narrow terrain of the battlefield to neutralize the numerical advantage of the Persian forces, forcing Darius III into a vulnerable position. At Gaugamela, on the other hand, Alexander adapted his tactics to the wide-open plains, outflanking the Persian army by using his cavalry to strike at the critical points of the Persian lines.

Tactical Innovation: Battle of Granicus, Issus, and Gaugamela

While Alexander's strategic genius is undeniable, it was his tactical brilliance that allowed him to achieve such spectacular victories. His ability to orchestrate complex maneuvers on the battlefield was unmatched.

The Battle of Granicus (334 BC)

The Battle of Granicus was Alexander's first major engagement in Asia and set the tone for his military campaigns. In this battle, he faced a much larger Persian force. However, Alexander's tactical brilliance lay in his rapid assault and the use of flanking maneuvers. By sending his cavalry around the flanks of the Persian army, he disrupted their formations and caused them to panic, leading to a decisive victory. The battle also marked the first significant clash with Persian forces, establishing Alexander's reputation as a fearless and innovative leader.

The Battle of Issus (333 BC)

The Battle of Issus is often considered one of Alexander's most impressive tactical victories. Despite being heavily outnumbered by the Persian army, Alexander used the terrain to his advantage, forcing Darius to fight in a narrow area where his superior numbers were less effective. In a brilliant move, Alexander's cavalry charged through a gap in the Persian lines, causing disarray and forcing Darius to retreat. The victory at Issus was not only a military triumph but also a psychological blow to the Persian king, demonstrating Alexander's ability to crush the morale of his enemies.

The Battle of Gaugamela (331 BC)

The Battle of Gaugamela was Alexander's greatest and final confrontation with Darius III. Despite facing a Persian army that was both numerically superior and better equipped, Alexander employed a well-coordinated combination of tactics to decisively defeat the Persians. By using his cavalry to outflank the Persian forces and attacking their weak points, he was able to create chaos within Darius's ranks. The battle demonstrated Alexander's ability to anticipate the movements of his enemies and to adapt his tactics to the specific conditions of the battlefield.

Leadership Style: Inspiration and Discipline

One of the key factors behind Alexander's success was his exceptional leadership style. He was not only a brilliant strategist but also a leader who inspired his men through his own actions, ensuring their loyalty and discipline. His leadership can be broken down into three key elements: personal example, charismatic authority, and fearless determination.

Leading by Example

Alexander's leadership was deeply personal. He led his troops from the front, often engaging directly in battle alongside them. This willingness to face the same dangers as his soldiers earned him their respect and admiration. At the Battle of Issus, for example, Alexander was at the forefront of the charge, his cavalry cutting through the Persian lines with precision. His fearlessness in battle made him a symbol of strength for his troops, and they were willing to follow him to the ends of the earth.

Charismatic Authority

Alexander's charisma played a crucial role in his ability to command such loyalty from his soldiers. He was able to inspire his men, not just through his actions, but through his speeches and personal connection with them. Unlike many rulers who maintained a physical distance from their soldiers, Alexander often interacted directly with his troops, engaging them with stories of their shared glory and promising them the spoils of conquest.

His ability to connect with his men also extended to his respect for local cultures. He adopted some Persian customs, for example, and even began to dress in Persian attire, a move that angered some of his Macedonian followers but showed his willingness to integrate diverse elements into his leadership style.

Fearless Determination

Alexander's determination and unyielding drive were critical to his success. He often pushed his men to their physical and mental limits, yet he was known for sharing in their hardships. His famous march across the Gedrosian Desert in 325 BC, which saw his army suffer immense hardship, was a testament to his ability to endure extreme conditions. Despite the relentless nature of his campaigns, Alexander's resolve never wavered. He believed deeply in his destiny, often referring to himself as the son of Zeus, and this sense of purpose motivated him to push forward, no matter the obstacle.

Influence on Later Generals: Caesar, Napoleon, and Modern Leaders

Alexander's military genius and leadership style would serve as a model for many of history's greatest military leaders. His undefeated record, tactical flexibility, and speed of campaign made him a touchstone for generals who sought to emulate his success.

Julius Caesar

Julius Caesar, one of history's most famous military leaders, was greatly influenced by Alexander. Caesar admired Alexander's ability to rapidly mobilize his forces and engage in decisive battles. Like Alexander, Caesar was known for leading his troops from the front, inspiring loyalty through his personal involvement in the battlefield. Caesar's conquest of Gaul and his campaigns during the Roman civil wars reflect a similar combination of speed, tactical flexibility, and psychological warfare that Alexander employed.

Napoleon Bonaparte

Napoleon Bonaparte also saw Alexander as a model of military leadership. Napoleon's campaigns, particularly his maneuver warfare and his ability to strike quickly and decisively, mirrored Alexander's approach. Both leaders were masters of grand strategy, able to unite vast territories under their rule through swift and overwhelming military action. Napoleon's admiration for Alexander extended to his own cavalry tactics and ability to move forces quickly, concepts that Napoleon would employ with devastating effect on the European battlefield.

Modern Generals

Modern generals, from Eisenhower to Patton, continue to study Alexander's campaigns for insight into logistics, tactical innovation, and leadership. The speed of Alexander's campaigns, his ability to adapt to different environments, and his effectiveness at mobilizing his troops are still relevant today in contemporary military strategy.

CHAPTER 14. MYTH AND MEMORY

The Legend of Alexander the Great

The story of Alexander the Great transcends the limits of historical record and transforms into a rich tapestry of myth, legend, and cultural memory. From the moment of his death, Alexander became more than just a historical figure; he evolved into an icon, a symbol of heroism, divinity, and conquest that was immortalized through the centuries. His legend was shaped by the cultures he encountered, the territories he conquered, and the ways in which his deeds were remembered and retold. The myths surrounding Alexander reveal much about the nature of hero worship, the intersection of East and West, and the continuing fascination with one of history's greatest figures.

Alexander in Eastern and Western Traditions

The contrasting ways in which Alexander has been remembered in the East and the West reflect the cultural and political landscapes of the societies that molded his image. While the Western world often framed Alexander as a heroic figure, glorifying his achievements and leadership, the Eastern traditions, particularly in Persia and the Indian subcontinent, shaped a more complex and multifaceted view of him, one that acknowledged his military genius but also framed him as a figure of destiny, divinity, and sometimes even as a conqueror to be both revered and feared.

Western Traditions: The Heroic Conqueror

In the Western world, Alexander's legacy was largely shaped by the Greek historian Plutarch, who wrote extensively about his life in his Parallel Lives. For Plutarch and many later historians, Alexander was viewed as the ultimate conqueror and a model of leadership and military strategy. His victories, his ability to inspire loyalty in his troops, and his unprecedented ability to conquer vast swathes of the known world made him a paragon of virtue and heroism.

Over the centuries, Alexander's image as the heroic conqueror was solidified in medieval Europe through the Alexander Romance, a collection of legendary tales that expanded on his historical achievements. In these tales, Alexander was portrayed as a godlike figure, often performing miraculous feats and engaging in adventures that went beyond the boundaries of historical fact. These stories were meant to glorify him and offer an idealized version of his life, emphasizing his greatness and his near-divine qualities.

Alexander's influence extended into Christian traditions as well, where he was seen as a precursor to Christ. In the Middle Ages, many Christian theologians and philosophers saw Alexander's conquests as divinely ordained, with his empire providing a framework for the spread of Christianity in later centuries. His campaigns were often interpreted as the fulfillment of divine will, allowing for the spread of the Gospel throughout the known world.

Even today, Alexander continues to be revered in the West as a symbol of military genius, ambition, and courage. His image has appeared in art, literature, and popular culture, from the works of Shakespeare and Byron to modern films and books. The Western tradition has largely focused on his heroic qualities, portraying him as a figure who, despite his flaws, embodied the ideals of glory, honor, and leadership.

Eastern Traditions: A God, a Hero, and a Conqueror

In the East, Alexander's image has been shaped by the cultures he encountered during his campaigns, particularly in Persia and India. His military successes were often viewed with awe, but they also led to a more nuanced and, at times, ambivalent view of his legacy. In Persian and Indian literature, Alexander was frequently portrayed as both a hero and a destroyer, a man who embodied both the divine and the tyrannical.

In Persia, Alexander's invasion and the fall of the Achaemenid Empire marked a traumatic chapter in the history of the Persian people. Yet, over time, he was integrated into the Persian historical narrative and was even admired as a great leader. The Shahnameh, the Persian epic, presents Alexander as a noble figure, but also as someone whose military success came at a great cost. Persian authors, particularly in the Sassanid period, began to refer to him as 'Iskander', a title that would be used throughout the Islamic world.

Alexander's portrayal in Persian literature highlights his imperial conquests, but it also acknowledges his visionary leadership. The image of Alexander as a conqueror, at once feared and respected, is a recurring theme in Persian poetry and historical accounts. His impact on Persian literature can be seen in the later works of Rudaki and other poets, who often depicted him as a ruler of extraordinary vision and ambition, though never as a purely heroic figure.

Indian Traditions: A Divine Hero

In India, Alexander's encounter with the Indian subcontinent was marked by his invasion of the Punjab and his famous battle with King Porus at the Hydaspes River in 326 BC. However, the significance of Alexander in Indian traditions is complex. In some Indian texts, Alexander was portrayed as a divine hero who was destined to conquer and spread the message of Greek culture. In others, he was seen as a tyrant, a conqueror whose empire was built on the subjugation of native peoples.

The Greco-Buddhist art of the Gandhara region reflects a blending of Greek and Indian influences, symbolizing the integration of Alexander's legacy into the Indian cultural fabric. Alexander's appearance in these artistic depictions, often as a noble figure in the context of Buddhism, suggests that he was seen as a figure of destiny, who played a key role in shaping the cultural and philosophical exchanges between East and West.

In the Indian subcontinent, the encounter with Alexander was also mythologized, and Alexander's character was imbued with divine qualities. He was sometimes seen as a figure who was sent by the gods to test the limits of human ambition and to open new paths for the flow of knowledge and culture. Some Indian texts even compare him to Hercules, suggesting that Alexander was seen as a quasi-divine figure whose military prowess and adventures rivaled those of the great heroes of legend.

The 'Alexander Romance' and Medieval Legends

One of the most enduring elements of Alexander's mythological legacy is the Alexander Romance, a collection of medieval legends that expanded upon the historical figure and transformed him into a near-mythical hero. The Alexander Romance was a series of stories written in Greek, Latin, and later in many European languages, which became widely popular during the Middle Ages.

The Alexander Romance did not focus solely on historical events but was a fantastical and often supernatural account of Alexander's life and adventures. It combined elements of romance, myth, and adventure, with tales of Alexander's encounters with gods, monsters, and wizards. The Romance portrayed him as a flawless hero whose deeds defied the normal limits of human achievement. Some versions of the Romance even suggested that Alexander was the son of Zeus, a belief that further elevated him to the status of a divine figure.

One of the most famous elements of the Alexander Romance is the story of his journey to the ends of the world, where he seeks the Water of Life and encounters mystical creatures. The legends associated with his military campaigns were expanded into fantastic tales of magic, divine intervention, and supernatural feats, helping to solidify Alexander's image as a legendary figure.

The medieval Alexander was not just a conqueror, but a figure who transcended the boundaries of the known world. His adventures, his interactions with gods and mythological creatures, and his ultimate quest for immortality turned him into an icon whose legacy was celebrated in literature, art, and oral traditions.

Alexander in the Qur'an and Persian Literature

In both Islamic and Persian traditions, Alexander's legacy was woven into a tapestry of myth and history, with him often depicted in ways that both admired and cautioned against the dangers of unchecked ambition.

In the Qur'an, Alexander is often identified with Dhul-Qarnayn, a mysterious and powerful ruler who is said to have traveled to the ends of the Earth to build a wall to protect against the Gog and Magog. The depiction of Dhul-Qarnayn in the Qur'an is largely positive, associating him with wisdom, justice, and divine will. However, the narrative also highlights his awareness of the limitations of his power and the importance of humility in the face of divine authority. In Islamic traditions, Alexander/Dhul-Qarnayn is not portrayed as a god, but as a powerful and benevolent ruler who served the will of God.

In Persian literature, the figure of Iskander (Alexander) was mythologized in the Shahnameh, where he is portrayed as a noble conqueror but also a tyrant who brought destruction to the Persian Empire. The Shahnameh's portrayal of Alexander is complex, while he is admired for his military prowess and leadership, he is also seen as someone whose actions caused irreparable harm to the Persian world.

Was He a God, a Hero, or a Tyrant?

The question of whether Alexander was a god, a hero, or a tyrant is one that has been debated for centuries. The answer depends on the perspective of the culture or tradition in question. In the West, Alexander was often elevated to the status of a heroic figure, embodying the ideal of greatness and virtue. In the East, particularly in Persian and Indian traditions, Alexander was seen as a more complex figure, one who was both revered for his leadership and achievements and feared for his destructive conquests.

In medieval legends and Islamic traditions, Alexander's divine attributes were often emphasized, suggesting that he was a figure of destiny whose actions were guided by the gods. However, even in these accounts, there was recognition of his human flaws and the limits of his power. Ultimately, Alexander's legacy is not confined to a single identity; rather, it is a blend of mythological elements, historical facts, and cultural interpretations that have shaped how he is remembered across time and space.

CHAPTER 15. FINAL REFLECTIONS

The Legacy of Alexander the Great

Alexander the Great's life was a whirlwind of ambition, conquest, and exploration, one that left an indelible mark on the history of the world. His name has become synonymous with empire-building, military brilliance, and the quest for immortality. But as we look back on his extraordinary achievements, we must also confront the complex reality of his short life and the unfinished dreams that ultimately defined his legacy. This final chapter of our exploration into the life of Alexander seeks to reflect on the full scope of his accomplishments, the limitations of his reign, the mystery that still surrounds him, and the reasons why his story continues to captivate the world today.

What Alexander Achieved: A Legacy of Empire and Cultural Fusion

By the time of his death in 323 BC, Alexander had achieved what few in history could even dream of: the creation of one of the largest empires the world had ever seen. His empire spanned from Macedon in the west to the Indus River in the east, a vast territory that included much of the Persian Empire, Egypt, and parts of India. This unparalleled confluence of lands not only expanded his realm but also created a unique fusion of cultures, beliefs, and traditions that has had a lasting impact on the world.

Conquests of the Known World

At the heart of Alexander's achievements was his incredible success as a military commander. His ability to lead armies across thousands of miles of varied terrain, defeating powerful enemies, and maintaining discipline and morale among his troops was extraordinary. His tactical brilliance, demonstrated in battles like Granicus, Issus, and Gaugamela, showcased his unparalleled ability to outmaneuver opponents, regardless of their size or strength.

Alexander's most significant military achievement was his defeat of the Persian Empire, which had been the dominant power in the ancient world for centuries.

His conquest of Darius III, the fall of Persian capitals such as Babylon, Susa, and Persepolis, and his subsequent establishment of his own cities, marked the definitive collapse of the Persian Empire and the rise of a new world order.

Alexander's military prowess wasn't limited to the battlefield. He was also a gifted strategist who understood the importance of psychological warfare and propaganda. He used these tools to inspire loyalty among his men, intimidate enemies, and secure his reputation as a near-divine conqueror. His speed of conquest, the ability to cover vast distances in record time, was a testament to his strategic foresight and ability to mobilize his forces effectively.

The Spread of Hellenistic Culture

Perhaps one of Alexander's most enduring achievements was his role in the spread of Hellenistic culture across three continents. As he expanded his empire, Alexander took it upon himself to integrate Greek culture with the diverse traditions of the lands he conquered. He founded cities, the most famous being Alexandria in Egypt, which would become a center of learning and culture in the ancient world.

In these cities, Greek language, philosophy, art, and architecture flourished. At the same time, Alexander encouraged the exchange of ideas and traditions between East and West, which led to the formation of the Hellenistic world. This era saw the blending of Greek and Persian, Egyptian, and Indian cultures, creating a dynamic and cosmopolitan society that transcended geographical boundaries.

Alexander's cultural vision was realized in the syncretism of religious practices, the spread of Greek philosophy, and the intermingling of artistic styles. While Alexander himself was never able to fully bring these elements together during his lifetime, his efforts set the stage for the subsequent Hellenistic kingdoms, where Greek influence would continue to shape the development of the ancient world for centuries.

What Alexander Failed to Achieve: The Limits of His Vision

Despite his extraordinary successes, there were many aspects of his vision that remained unfulfilled, and these limitations form a critical part of his legacy.

Alexander's ambitious plans, which had no true precedent in history, eventually faltered due to the practical constraints of his empire and his untimely death.

The Conquest of Arabia and Further East

One of the key elements of Alexander's vision was the conquest of Arabia and the continuing expansion of his empire into the far reaches of India and beyond. After his victory at Gaugamela, Alexander had set his sights on the Arabian Peninsula and had planned a campaign that would have extended his empire even further. He was also contemplating further exploration into Central Asia, reaching into areas that were barely known to the Greeks, including regions beyond the Indus.

However, Alexander's plans for further conquests were derailed by the exhaustion of his troops. After years of relentless campaigning, Alexander's army, long accustomed to fighting and marching without respite, began to mutiny, unwilling to march further into the unknown territories of the east. His soldiers, many of whom had been with him since the beginning of his journey, refused to continue after the battle of the Hyphasis River (326 BC), and Alexander, reluctantly, turned back.

This failure to conquer Arabia and press on into India's interior is often seen as one of the greatest unfulfilled ambitions of Alexander's reign. Though he had demonstrated remarkable military and strategic brilliance, the sheer logistical challenge of maintaining a campaign in the vast, unfamiliar territories of the Middle East and Asia ultimately proved beyond his grasp.

Consolidation of His Empire

Even more significant than Alexander's unfulfilled conquests was the issue of consolidating his empire. Despite the grandeur of his military achievements, Alexander struggled to integrate the vast regions he had conquered into a cohesive empire. His efforts at administrative reform were sporadic and uncoordinated, and after his death, his empire fractured into several competing Hellenistic kingdoms.

Though he appointed satraps and founded cities to administer his empire, Alexander did not live long enough to establish a lasting governance structure or ensure his empire's political stability. His vision of cultural fusion, blending Greek and local traditions, was only partially realized, and many of the regions he conquered remained, to some extent, resistant to Greek influence.

Had Alexander lived longer, he may have been able to build a more sustainable empire, one that could have endured and perhaps even integrated the diverse peoples he conquered. But without a clear succession plan or a solid political structure in place, his empire crumbled in the wake of his sudden death.

The Enduring Mystery and Magnetism of His Story

Part of the reason that Alexander the Great continues to captivate us is the mystery surrounding his life, his death, and the legacy he left behind. Alexander's rapid rise and untimely death have inspired endless speculation about his character, motivations, and the true nature of his ambition.

The Mystery of His Death

Theories abound as to the cause of his death: was it fever caused by malaria, as many historians suggest? Did he die from the effects of poisoning, whether at the hands of political rivals or even by his own bodyguards? Was he simply worn out by the endless pressures of ruling such a vast empire?

Alexander's sudden death, at the age of 32, left a power vacuum and an array of unanswered questions. The lack of a clear heir added to the intrigue surrounding his passing. Why did he die so young? What could he have accomplished had he lived another decade or more? These questions have contributed to the ongoing fascination with his life and the world of possibilities that died with him.

The Charismatic Leader

Another element of the mystery of Alexander's legacy is the charismatic leadership that he exuded. He was a man capable of inspiring extraordinary loyalty in his troops, even in the face of extreme hardship. His ability to inspire devotion and respect, to lead with both vision and bravery, has made him an enduring figure in leadership studies.

Many modern leaders, military and political, continue to study Alexander's methods of inspiring loyalty, mobilizing troops, and maintaining discipline even in the most challenging of circumstances. Alexander was not just a brilliant general; he was a leader in the truest sense of the word, and his magnetism is part of what makes him such a compelling figure.

Why Alexander Still Captivates the World Today

The legend of Alexander the Great is one that continues to inspire and fascinate people today, nearly two and a half millennia after his death. But why does his story continue to captivate us in the modern world?

The Universal Appeal of Heroism

At its core, Alexander's story is one of heroism, the pursuit of greatness, the drive to achieve the seemingly impossible, and the ability to inspire others through courage, ambition, and sacrifice. These qualities are timeless, and they resonate with people across cultures and eras. In a world that often seems dominated by obstacles and limitations, the figure of Alexander, bold, daring, and uncompromising in his goals, offers a powerful ideal to strive for.

The Legacy of Empire and Cultural Exchange

Moreover, Alexander's legacy as the builder of a vast empire that connected East and West continues to have a significant impact on global history. His empire, while short-lived, laid the foundation for a cultural exchange that shaped the subsequent development of both the Greek and Persian worlds, as well as influencing India, the Middle East, and Europe. The ideals of Hellenism, the fusion of Greek and Eastern cultures, continue to be felt in modern politics, philosophy, and society.

The Mystery of His Character

Finally, the mystery surrounding Alexander's personality, his character, and the true nature of his ambitions continues to inspire endless discussion. Was he a god, a tyrant, or a hero? Did he view himself as a divine figure, or was he simply driven by the desire for power and glory? These questions ensure that Alexander's legacy remains as enigmatic as it is inspiring.

The Enduring Impact of Alexander the Great

Alexander the Great remains one of the most compelling figures in human history. His achievements were extraordinary, but so too were his failures. His quest for greatness and his unrelenting drive left a legacy that continues to shape our understanding of leadership, power, and empire-building. As we reflect on his life, we are reminded not only of the remarkable feats he accomplished but also of the limits of his vision, limits that were imposed by time, circumstance, and his untimely death.

Yet it is the mystery of Alexander, his magnetism, and the grandness of his vision that ensure his story continues to captivate us today.

EPILOGUE: A DREAM OUTLIVES ITS DREAMER

Alexander the Great's life story is one of exceptional ambition, unparalleled achievement, and untimely death. His story is not just about the grand expanse of territory he conquered, nor the profound cultural impact he had. His story is also one of mortality, of a man who rose to unimaginable heights only to have his empire fragment almost immediately after his death. In many ways, Alexander was the embodiment of the human paradox: a man who sought to conquer time and space, but whose life was cut short before his dreams could be fully realized.

In this epilogue, we reflect on the impermanence of all things, the rise and fall of empires, the fleeting nature of life, and the legacy left by those who dare to dream beyond the limits of the possible. Alexander's mortality and his ambition serve as a timeless reminder of the balance between greatness and the inevitable consequences that come with the pursuit of power. His legacy, however, lives on, shaping the world in profound ways. His relevance in the modern world continues to inspire, challenge, and serve as a cautionary tale. In the end, we come to understand that greatness always comes at a cost, whether the price is paid in human life, sacrifice, or the burden of history.

Reflections on Mortality, Ambition, and Empire

Alexander the Great's achievements were so extraordinary that they have often obscured the fact that, like all mortals, he was subject to the inexorable passage of time. He was 32 years old when he died in 323 BC, an age when most people would be at the height of their lives. But for Alexander, this age represented the premature end of a life that had burned so brightly, yet for so short a time.

His death marked the end of an era. The empire he had forged, one that stretched across continents and embodied the grandest ambitions of a single man, did not last long after his passing. His body was barely cold when his generals, his Diadochi, fought among themselves for control over the pieces of his fractured empire. The unity Alexander had strived to build through his conquests and vision dissipated almost overnight. His plans to create a lasting empire, one that transcended national borders and fused East with West, crumbled without him.

Yet, in his mortality, Alexander's story became even more poignant. Death, after all, is the great equalizer, and no matter how powerful or grand the empire, every mortal ruler must eventually confront it. The fact that he died so young, just when his ambitions seemed most within reach, is one of the factors that have contributed to the mystique surrounding his life. It has allowed for an ongoing narrative of what he could have accomplished, how much further he could have pushed the boundaries of his empire, how much more he could have shaped the world.

In this light, Alexander's death reminds us that the pursuit of greatness is always subject to the limitations of the human condition. Ambition, no matter how grand, has its limits, and the very impermanence of life ensures that even the greatest of empires will eventually fall. As much as Alexander sought immortality, his life itself was a reminder of the fleeting nature of all things, including empires, ideas, and even the most charismatic leaders.

Alexander's Relevance in the Modern World

Although Alexander's empire fractured within a few years of his death, his influence endures through time, shaping the world in ways that still resonate today. From the spread of Hellenistic culture to the ideals of empire, Alexander's legacy has influenced leaders, thinkers, and empires throughout history and continues to have relevance in the modern world.

Even in the modern world, Alexander's legacy continues to shape Western thought. His conquests spread Greek philosophy, particularly the ideas of Plato and Aristotle, across the known world, and the echoes of these philosophies continue to influence political, ethical, and philosophical thought today. Leaders and scholars still look to Alexander's ambition, his vision of a unified world, and his ability to incorporate different cultures as lessons in leadership and diplomacy.

The Myth of Empire and Leadership

Alexander's empire-building also left an indelible mark on the idea of what it means to be an empire-builder. His campaigns and his vision of a unified world continue to inspire modern political leaders, many of whom reference Alexander as a model of military and political success. His strategic brilliance and the speed with which he conquered territory have become central themes in military studies.

At the same time, Alexander's story raises complex questions about the nature of empire. His conquests were not just about military victory; they were about a vision of a world united under one banner, one that incorporated both conquest and culture. This idea of an empire that blends diverse peoples and ideas has echoed throughout history and continues to challenge leaders today in terms of the balance between coercion and integration, dominance and cultural exchange.

In the modern world, Alexander's legacy has been invoked both as a model to emulate and as a warning. The consequences of empire-building, whether the destruction of local cultures, the subjugation of peoples, or the costs of war, are just as significant today as they were in Alexander's time. In this way, Alexander's rise and fall continue to speak to the challenges facing modern-day leaders who seek power, territory, and influence in an interconnected world.

The Idea That Greatness Always Comes at a Cost

Perhaps the most important reflection from Alexander's life is the realization that greatness, whether in war, empire-building, or cultural achievement, always comes at a cost. For Alexander, that cost was both personal and global.

On a personal level, Alexander's insatiable ambition demanded sacrifices that weighed heavily on his own life and the lives of those around him. His relentless military campaigns took a toll on his body, his relationships, and his sanity. His men, though fiercely loyal, were often pushed to their limits, enduring long marches, battles, and hardships in foreign lands. Alexander's death, though shrouded in mystery, can be seen as a tragic consequence of a life lived with such intensity and unyielding ambition.

On a larger scale, Alexander's empire-building required the destruction of many cultures and peoples. His conquest of the Persian Empire meant the decimation of the ancient Persian state, the destruction of Persepolis, and the subjugation of millions of people. His invasion of India led to widespread death and suffering, both among his own soldiers and the local populations. Even as he sought to blend and integrate cultures, his expansion was also marked by violence, destruction, and the imposition of foreign rule.

This fragility of empire, how quickly it can dissolve after the death of a powerful leader, serves as a reminder that the foundations of greatness are often built on unstable ground. The power and prestige of Alexander's empire were temporary, and his empire's legacy was ultimately defined by the splintering that followed.

Moreover, the personal costs to Alexander himself, his mental and emotional strain, his guilt, and the toll of his unrelenting drive for power, make us question whether the pursuit of greatness is worth the sacrifice. In many ways, Alexander's life asks a fundamental question that resonates throughout history: What price is too high for greatness?

A Dream That Outlived Its Dreamer

The life of Alexander the Great is a study of a visionary whose ambition exceeded the limits of his own lifetime. He sought not only to conquer the world but to shape it in his own image, to create an empire that would endure and unite the known world under the banner of Hellenistic ideals. His achievements were monumental, but they came at a cost, and his untimely death revealed the fragility of empire, the impermanence of power, and the inevitable nature of mortality.

In the end, Alexander's legacy is a dream that outlived its dreamer. Though his empire fragmented and his conquests were undone by the passage of time, his influence continues to shape the world today. His ambition, his victories, and his failures speak to the eternal human desire for greatness and the complex consequences of that pursuit. Alexander's story is a powerful reminder that greatness always carries with it a cost, and that no matter how grand the dream, it is always subject to the limits of time, mortality, and human frailty.

APPENDIX

Glossary of People, Places and Terms

This glossary provides essential terms and references that are frequently encountered when studying Alexander the Great's life, campaigns, and impact.

People & Titles

- Alexander the Great – King of Macedon (r. 336–323 BC), son of Philip II and Olympias. One of history's greatest military commanders and empire-builders.

- Philip II – Alexander's father and predecessor as King of Macedon. A skilled diplomat and military innovator who unified Greece under Macedonian rule.

- Olympias – Alexander's mother, a Molossian princess of Epirus, known for her intense religiosity and ambition for her son.

- Aristotle – Greek philosopher and scientist, student of Plato and tutor to Alexander. He greatly influenced Alexander's worldview and interest in knowledge.

- Darius III – The last king of the Achaemenid Persian Empire, defeated by Alexander at Issus and Gaugamela.

- Roxana (Roxane) – Bactrian noblewoman and Alexander's first wife. Their son, Alexander IV, was killed after Alexander's death.

- Hephaestion – Alexander's closest friend, general, and possibly lover. His death in 324 BC deeply affected Alexander.

- The Diadochi – 'Successors'; the generals and companions of Alexander who divided his empire after his death.

Major Battles & Campaigns

- Battle of Chaeronea (338 BC) – Decisive victory by Philip II and Alexander over the Greek city-states of Athens and Thebes.

- Battle of Granicus (334 BC) – Alexander's first major battle against the Persian satraps of Asia Minor.

- Battle of Issus (333 BC) – Victory over Darius III in Cilicia; Alexander gained control of Syria and the eastern Mediterranean.

- Siege of Tyre (332 BC) – A seven-month siege of the Phoenician island city; Alexander built a causeway to reach and destroy the city.

- Battle of Gaugamela (331 BC) – The decisive battle against Darius III, which led to the fall of the Persian Empire.

- Battle of the Hydaspes (326 BC) – Fought in India against King Porus. Despite war elephants and difficult terrain, Alexander triumphed.

- Mutiny at the Hyphasis (Beas) River (326 BC) – Alexander's troops refused to continue eastward into India, forcing him to turn back.

Geographical Regions & Cities

- Macedon (Macedonia) – The ancient kingdom in northern Greece from which Alexander launched his conquests.

- Pella – Capital of Macedon and Alexander's birthplace.

- Achaemenid Empire – The Persian Empire overthrown by Alexander, stretching from Anatolia to the Indus Valley.

- Asia Minor (Anatolia) – Modern-day Turkey; the first region conquered by Alexander in his Persian campaign.

- Hellespont (Dardanelles) – Narrow strait between Europe and Asia. Alexander crossed it in 334 BC to begin his invasion of Persia.

- Babylon – A major ancient city in Mesopotamia. Alexander made it his imperial capital and died there in 323 BC.

- Susa – Persian administrative capital, captured by Alexander after Gaugamela.

- Persepolis – Ceremonial capital of Persia, looted and burned by Alexander in 330 BC.

- Alexandria – The most famous of the many cities founded by Alexander, located in Egypt. It became a center of learning and Hellenistic culture.

- Siwa Oasis – In the Egyptian desert, site of the Oracle of Zeus-Ammon, where Alexander was declared a divine son.

- Bactria – Region in modern Afghanistan; the site of fierce resistance and Alexander's marriage to Roxana.

- Sogdiana – Region of Central Asia; known for difficult terrain and stubborn resistance to Alexander's rule.

- Gedrosian Desert – Harsh desert in modern southern Iran and Pakistan. Alexander's disastrous march through it cost many lives.

- Hindu Kush – Mountain range crossed by Alexander during his invasion of the Indian subcontinent.

- Indus River – Major river in present-day Pakistan; Alexander's easternmost boundary before turning back.

- Hyphasis (Beas) River – The furthest point of Alexander's march into India, where his army refused to go farther.

Key Concepts & Terms

- Hellenism / Hellenistic Culture – The blending of Greek culture with that of the Middle East, Central Asia, and Egypt, encouraged by Alexander's conquests.

- Phalanx – The dominant Greek infantry formation, used extensively and innovatively by Alexander.

- Satrap – Provincial governor in the Persian Empire. Alexander often retained local satraps in conquered territories.

- Oracle of Ammon (Siwa) – A temple where Alexander was proclaimed the 'Son of Zeus-Ammon,' reinforcing his divine status.

- Proskynesis – A Persian custom of bowing or prostrating before the king, controversially introduced by Alexander into his court.

- Deification – Alexander encouraged the idea of his own divinity, being hailed as a god or demigod by various cultures.

- Diadochi Wars – Series of conflicts among Alexander's generals following his death, leading to the division of his empire.

- Stoicism & Epicureanism – Philosophical movements that flourished in the Hellenistic world shaped by Alexander's legacy.

Quotes Attributed to Alexander the Great

On Ambition and Conquest

"There is nothing impossible to him who will try."
A declaration of determination and vision, often cited to reflect Alexander's belief in human potential and willpower.

"I am not afraid of an army of lions led by a sheep; I am afraid of an army of sheep led by a lion."

A quote that captures Alexander's view of leadership and the decisive role of commanders in war.

"With the right strategy, courage, and timing, few can do what many cannot."
Though the exact origin is debated, this echoes his military philosophy.

"I would rather live a short life of glory than a long one of obscurity."
Reflects his deep commitment to achieving eternal fame, even at the cost of his life.

On Legacy and Greatness

"When we give someone our time, we actually give a portion of our life that we will never take back."
Often attributed to Alexander to highlight the value of time and personal presence, though its authenticity is debated.

"Heaven cannot brook two suns, nor earth two masters."
Allegedly said to Darius III, king of Persia, indicating that only one of them could rule the known world.

"Remember upon the conduct of each depends the fate of all."
A quote emphasising discipline, unity, and the importance of individual duty within the army.

On War and Leadership

"In the end, when it's over, all that matters is what you've done."
Reflects the pragmatism behind his drive to achieve lasting impact.

"My treasure lies in my soldiers' belly."
Said when asked about hoarding wealth, showing his emphasis on feeding and rewarding his troops.

"I am indebted to my father for living, but to my teacher for living well."
Refers to Philip II and Aristotle, revealing his respect for education and philosophy.

On Death and Mortality

"Bury my body, and do not build any monument. Keep my hands outside so that the world knows that the man who won the world had nothing in hand when he died."
A powerful (though likely legendary) deathbed instruction, symbolizing the futility of material ambition.

"To the strongest."
Alleged response when asked on his deathbed who should succeed him. This phrase launched the Wars of the Diadochi.

On Empire and Cultural Integration

"I do not distinguish between Greeks and barbarians."
Reportedly said in defense of his policy of cultural fusion and integration across his empire.

"God must have loved Afghans because he made them so beautiful."
Sometimes attributed to Alexander during his campaigns in Bactria, though its authenticity is uncertain and likely apocryphal.

"An empire is conquered by the sword but ruled by the mind."
Reflects his ideal of combining military force with political wisdom and diplomacy.

Possibly Misattributed or Apocryphal

These quotes are widely circulated but are often considered dubious or of later origin, though they still capture the mythos of Alexander:

"When Alexander saw the breadth of his domain, he wept for there were no more worlds to conquer."
Popularized by Roman sources and later by literature and film, but not found in early Greek accounts.

"A tomb now suffices for him for whom the whole world was not sufficient."
Said by the Roman writer Juvenal, reflecting on the irony of Alexander's mortality.

Cities Founded by and Named After Alexander

- **Alexandria, located in modern day Alexandria, Egypt**
  The most famous; founded in 331 BCE; became major center of Hellenistic culture.

- **Alexandria Arachosia, located in modern day Kandahar, Afghanistan**
  Key eastern outpost; linked to Persian and Indian routes.

- **Alexandria Arion, possibly located in modern day Herat, Afghanistan**

- **Alexandria on the Oxus, located near modern day Ai-Khanoum, Afghanistan**
  Strategic city on the Oxus River (Amu Darya).

- **Alexandria in Margiana, located near modern day Merv, Turkmenistan**
  A defensive garrison town in Central Asia.

- **Alexandria Eschate, located in modern day Khujand, Tajikistan**
  'Alexandria the Furthest', the easternmost outpost.

- **Alexandria Bucephala, located near modern day Jhelum, Pakistan**
  Named after his horse Bucephalus after the Battle of Hydaspes.

- **Alexandria Nicaea, located near modern day Jhelum, Pakistan**
  Possibly opposite Bucephala; 'Victory Alexandria'.

- **Alexandria on the Indus, located near modern day Uch or Bahawalpur, Pakistan**
  Founded during his campaign toward the Indian Ocean.

- **Alexandria Carmania, possibly near modern day Kerman, Iran**
  Established on return from India.

- **Alexandria Susiana, located near modern day Susa, Iran**
  Administrative post in Elam.

- **Alexandria Prophthasia, located in modern day Farah, Afghanistan**
  Means 'forewarning', founded after a plot was discovered.

- **Alexandria in Ariana, located near modern day Herat or in western Afghanistan**
  One of several in the eastern satrapies.

- **Alexandria in the Caucasus, located near modern day Kabul, Afghanistan**
  Important route between India and Bactria.

- **Alexandria Troas, located near modern day Dalyan, Turkey (Aegean coast)**
  A port city later developed by successors.

- **Alexandria ad Issum, located near modern day İskenderun, Turkey**

Founded after Battle of Issus, 333 BCE.

- **Alexandropolis, located near modern day modern Edessa, Greece**
  First city founded by Alexander (before Asia campaign).

- **Alexandria Rhambacia, possibly located in modern day southern Pakistan**
  One of the cities founded on the return from India.

- **Alexandria Orietai, located near modern day Bela, Pakistan**

- **Alexandria in Egypt (Siwa), located near modern day Siwa Oasis, Egypt**
  Not a city per se, but his visit to Siwa helped solidify divine legitimacy.

ABOUT THE AUTHOR

I am a passionate military and history writer whose love for the past was kindled by family stories. One grandfather endured four years as a prisoner of war in Poland during World War 2, while my great-grandfather fought at the Somme in World War 1 — a legacy that ignited a lifelong fascination with courage, conflict, and the human spirit in wartime.

In 2024, after receiving a diagnosis of stage 4 cancer, I turned to writing with newfound purpose. The act of storytelling has become a welcome distraction for me! As of July 2025, I've completed 34 cycles of fortnightly chemotherapy, a treatment that continues — but so does my writing, undeterred and determined.

Whether I'm exploring the battles of World War II, the legends of Greek mythology, the intrigue of Roman emperors, or the ambition of Alexander the Great, I write to inspire curiosity in readers, both young and old, and make history come alive with meaning.

I live in the Cotswolds with my wife, my two children, and two lovely black Labradors. When not writing or reading, you'll likely find me wandering the hills dreaming up my next journey into the past.

See more at: ***james-burrows.com and @burrowsauthor***.

If you enjoyed this book, I'd appreciate a review – please scan the QR Code below:

If you'd like to read more, you can find all my books at: